Our World of Things

Our World of Things

Patricia A. Reuse

A Stewardship Challenge for Your Life

BROADMAN PRESS
Nashville, Tennessee

4252-46

ISBN: 0-8054-5246-X

Dewey Decimal Classification: 248.6

Subject Heading: STEWARDSHIP

Library of Congress Catalog Card Number: 84-12705

Printed in the United States of America

Library of Congress Cataloging in Publication Data

Reuse, Patricia A., 1944-
Our world of things.

1. Stewardship, Christian. 2. Christian giving.
I. Title.
BV772.R46 1985 248'.6 84-12705
ISBN 0-8054-5246 (pbk.)

To my caring family, Ron and Lauren, who tolerated me through some rough times and prayed me through the ordeal of a first book

Acknowledgments

Special thanks go to those who granted permission for the use of poetry, lyrics, and illustrations for this book: James Dobson, Gary Davis, Douglas Pilot, and Joyce Shutt.

My appreciation also goes to my pastor, Arne Gulbrandsen, who provided some of the books and commentaries that I used, and to friends, who offered their prayer support.

I owe a great deal to my co-workers who, without complaining, put up with my frequent absences from work for an extended period of time in order that I could complete this project on time.

I also want to thank Michael Helman, who graciously did much of the typing and retyping, which was a tremendous help to me. Time is so precious.

Preface

I would like to write a book that would make people feel good about themselves for having read it. But I can't. Because what the Lord has pointed out in my own life, I see in the lives of other Christians. I could say if we're saved, it doesn't really matter how we spend our money: that is just a temporal concern. But it does matter. Jesus says that it does.

So I write to my brothers and sisters in Christ, who, like me, are affluent by the standards of world economy (not necessarily by our own), in hopes of sharing with you some of the concerns that I have for us, the contemporary church in an affluent society.

My purposes for writing this book are eightfold.

First, I hope to describe the materialistic society in which we as North Americans live and to demonstrate the invasion of this materialism in our lives individually as Christians and collectively as the church. I believe as a whole, Christians are unconscious of the vast role "things" play in our lives.

Second, I want to show that our materialistic lifestyle is not in line with what we say we believe about God's ownership and our stewardship. All of what we have is a gift from God. It seems to me that many of us are giving a tenth to the Lord and spending the other nine tenths on ourselves.

Third, I want to examine some of the reasons that we Christians give and some reasons we don't give.

Fourth, I want to show the gap between our own high standard of living and that of our less fortunate neighbors. We claim to serve a Lord who said, "You shall love your neighbor as yourself" (Mark 12:31). This command of Jesus was second only to the command to "love the Lord your God with all your heart, and with all your soul, and with all your mind, and with all your strength" (v. 30), and cannot authentically be separated from it in our Christian lives. The God-given realization of the sharp dichotomy in my own life-style between profession and action was the seed from which this book germinated. The Lord led me to wonder how people could believe we loved them if our compassion and giving didn't show it.

Fifth, I want to look at why Christians need to be different and why we need to be compassionate, sharing people.

Sixth, I would like to examine the differences between what we *need* and what we *want,* and provide some suggestions for living more simply. When affluent Christians live more simply, we will free money for preaching the gospel and meeting other human needs.

Next, I want to provide a list of avenues of helping and giving that will be useful in our personal lives, in our churches, in our communities, and in our world.

Finally, I want to challenge us to allow God to do something *new* in our lives in the area of stewardship even though we may have been Christians for years.

Contents

Our World of Things

The world is too much with us;
late and soon,
Getting and spending, we lay waste
our powers;
Little we see in nature that is ours.
—William Wordsworth

If the world were represented by one hundred people, six of them would be Americans. These six would consume 50 percent of the world's income. To say that we are a nation of consumers is an understatement. For example, the average North American consumes a ton of grain a year, five times that which the average person in a less-developed nation consumes. Rich nations currently feed their livestock more grain than is consumed directly by the people of India and China—who are more than one third of the human race.[1]

In few countries in the world is there such an abundance of consumer goods readily available to its citizenry as in America. Not only do we have "a chicken in every pot," but many have a microwave oven, a dishwasher, and a self-cleaning oven in the kitchen. We may have an ice maker, two television sets (at least one color, of course), a freezer in the basement, and two cars in the garage. We may have wall-to-wall carpet, a family room with a fireplace, a stereo, and a tape player. We have air conditioning for the summer and, if we live in the North, a wood stove for the winter.

The wood stove, which is truly an energy saver, is something of a return to the rustic, simple life, which I expect, we now miss. It means, though, that we must either buy wood or purchase a high-powered chain saw and maybe one of those handy new log splitters to cut our own.

Our rampant consumerism doesn't stop there. We live in the age of the home microcomputer so we add a whole new realm of "toys" to our growing list. We have traded traditional games like Scrabble, Clue, and Boggle for the more expensive computer games like Pac-man, Burger Time, and A-Mazeing. A videocassette recorder is a boon to those who would watch recent films in their homes and record television shows that they might have missed otherwise. Of course, we have electric slow cookers, electric skillets, food processors, electric knives, foot fixers, and all those other wonderful conveniences.

The things we possess are just one of many indicators of our never-ending consumerism.

Another indicator of our country's feverish desire to have things was illustrated by an article in *Time* magazine, "The American Way of Debt" (May 31, 1982). According to the article easy living on easy credit is getting millions into trouble. Our wallets are full of plastic cards. It's too easy to get what we want. We have forgotten how to wait for the things we really want. Instead, we want it all *now;* our fast-food culture may just be a symbol of our whole way of life. Can we blame our predicament on easy credit, or can we blame the root of the problem on our overwhelming desire to have it all, and to have it all *now?*

The fact that more stores are open seven days a week or twenty-four hours a day is a symptom of our disease of consumerism. Blue laws have faded and many more people are working on Sundays because employers find it profitable. It wouldn't be profitable if people weren't out there buying. We are twenty-four hour, seven-day-a-week consumers.

Sometimes material things are like drugs; they become habit-forming. The more we have, the more we seem to need to be satisfied (Eccl. 5:10). I have observed that possessions seem to come in groups; each one demands another. Let me illustrate. Some years ago we purchased a fireplace insert for the purpose of conserving fuel and fuel bills and still keeping a cold family member warm. For the most efficient use of the insert, we were required to buy at extra cost a blower to blow the hot air out into the room. Rather than pay high prices for wood, my husband decided to cut his own. A new chain saw became a necessity. Not having a fireproof mat in front of the insert to catch any flying ashes would have been foolhardy, so we bought one. Wood chips and debris constantly surrounded the hearth so my husband brought home our next toy: a Dustbuster. I could see what was happening at the time; I even commented about it. But I felt helpless to stop it. I see this same phenomenon occuring with the coming of home computers. A family buys a basic home computer (because they are educational), and begins a long journey of buying as the family sees the need for more advanced computer equipment and more and more expensive cartridges. Most of us have probably experienced this kind of "more and more" buying in our lives at some time or another.

Of course, advertising plays an important role in our rate of consumption. Concerning advertising, John Taylor, in his book, *Enough Is Enough*, says,

> Yet the significant fact is that producers, who are not accustomed to throwing good money after bad, continue to spend more and more astronomical figures on advertising. They believe that it accomplishes something. And of course they are right. Advertising helps enormously to create the consumer mood. It keeps things, and the value of getting things, continually before the public's eye.[2]

Another indicator of our consumerism would be a look at our own budgets, if we have one. Consider for a few moments what you spend your money on. How much of your income do you spend on yourself and your family? What kinds of things you do spend money on? Are they all necessary? How much besides the one tenth you give to your church goes to meet the needs of others?

Every year between October and December much comment is made about how we have allowed Christmas to become so commercialized. Then we tell ourselves it's what we believe about Christmas that counts. No matter what we Christians may say or believe about what Christmas really is, I expect we spend much more time shopping, spending, and wrapping than we do worshiping.

In our affluence, we have also become a nation of collectors. People collect everything from arrowheads to Wedgewood. There are countless books on the market telling people what to look for at flea markets and auctions, how to bid for various items, how to deal with appraisers, which items are valuable, and how to tell the difference. There are even encyclopedias of collectibles and books that encourage us to look for "gold" in our attics. Collecting may give us a reason for buying rather than giving, and, if so, it may not be a very good one.

Another indicator might be that we spend most of our income. Although I am not making a point for savings, we should note that Americans save approximately 6 percent of their incomes while Europeans tend to save 12 to 14 percent of what may be smaller incomes. How does our income compare with some other countries of the world? Let's look at some figures:

Per Capita Income for 1983[3]

Canada	10,296	New Zealand	7,363
Sweden	9,274	East Germany	5,340
Austria	9,114	Israel	3,332
United States	8,612	Soviet Union	2,600

Argentina	2,331	North Korea	570
Bulgaria	2,100	China	566
Malta	2,036	Grenada	500
Portugal	2,000	Zambia	414
Chile	1,950	India	200
Turkey	1,140	Afghanistan	168
Ecuador	1,050	Vietnam	150
Philippines	779	Bangladesh	105

This is just a sampling of the world's countries. You will immediately see that there are a few other countries that share a high standard of living with the United States, such as Canada and Austria, but, for the most part, the income for the majority of the world's people is far below adequate. Many of the underdeveloped countries are in desperate straits.

> During this century, while the world's population was growing 150 percent, the consumption of the world's most basic food was growing 650 percent. This growth of consumption can be traced directly to the affluence of a few nations. The average American consumes 3,240 calories a day. Sixty percent of the world's population consumes less than 2,200 calories, the critical minimum for an adequate diet. Grain-fed beef, grain-produced alcohol, and obesity as a national health problem all are signs of a selfishly indulgent society in the midst of a hungry world.[4]

Yes, obesity is another symptom of an overindulgent culture. Two of every three Americans are overweight. We live in a country where food is easily attainable, as close as our refrigerators, supermarket, or fast-food restaurant. Fortunately, we live in a culture where, for most of us, money for food is not scarce either. Consequently, we are a nation of dieters; the availability of food from morning till night has become something of a curse to our waistlines.

Am I saying that possessions are evil? No, all that God made was good (Gen. 1:31). Jesus was not an ascetic either. He attended marriage celebrations and dined with the prosperous.

The Bible warns us of the dangers of possessions. Possessions tempt us to forsake God (Deut. 8:7-18). Possessions tend make us blind to the needs of the poor (Luke 16:19-21). Possessions can lead to strife (Luke 12:13). Possessions and striving after them can become, consciously or unconsciously, the main purpose of our lives (Matt. 6:25; Luke 12:15-20). It is evident that most Christians in the Northern Hemisphere don't believe Jesus' teaching about the dangers of possessions. We have decided that covetousness is not as sinful as idolatry and adultery.

God has certainly blessed us as a nation, although we do have those who are poor and needy. Because of the relative wealth that we are blessed with as North Americans, I do have several real concerns for us as Christians.

Some Concerns

First, I am concerned that *things play an inordinate role in our lives* whether we are willing to admit it or not.

James Dobson, in his *Focus on the Family* film series, tells a story to illustrate how quickly the things he owns own him.

> Some time ago I moved into a new office and asked for the assistance of an interior decorator in buying furniture. He suggested I put something special on one particular wall. I asked what he had in mind. He said he thought a chimer clock would look good. I told him a chimer clock costs quite a lot, but he said, "I think it will look good there." I agreed that we'd get a chimer clock.
>
> We bought a beautiful Regulator Clock, but that thing has been broken three times in the past two years. Now, what does that mean? Every time the clock breaks, I have to go through files, find the warranty, locate the service center, pack the silly thing in a crate, get it in the car, haul it to a repair shop, hassle with the repairman when he doesn't fix it, and take it back when it breaks again. This has happened three times so far, and it is still not working. I was counseling a lady recently, and at 2:00 PM the clock chimed 10:00. That is the price of ownership. It has taken too much of my time; perhaps a half day of my life has gone into that chimer clock.
>
> What a waste! If I were to know how many days

> I'm allotted on this earth, I wonder how many of them . . . what percent . . . have I given to that chimer clock? I'm beginning to see all materialism that way, and I'm aware that everything I own eventually owns me.[5]

What price do we pay for ownership? Not only do things take time and energy to maintain and enjoy, but our possessions make us increasingly immobile. We think we are using things, when, in reality, things may be using us. We may be used up by the time we invest in things rather than people.

Jesus said, "Take heed, and beware of all covetousness; for a man's life does not consist in the abundance of his possessions" (Luke 12:15). I'm convinced that none of us as Christians believes that our primary purpose in life is to accumulate possessions. But do we tend to live as if that were true? We can only answer for ourselves.

Is it possible that we are like the rich man whose land brought forth plentifully?

> And he thought to himself, "What shall I do, for I have nowhere to store my crops?" And he said, "I will do this; I will pull down my barns, and build larger ones; and there I will store all . . . my goods. And I will say to my soul, Soul, you have ample goods laid up for many years; take your ease, eat, drink, be merry." But God said to him, "Fool! This night your soul is required of you; and the things you have prepared, whose will they be?" So is he

who lays up treasure for himself, and is not rich toward God (Luke 12:16-21).

Have we fooled ourselves about where our treasure is? Have we spent a substantial proportion of our time working for, accumulating, and enjoying "things"? Do we *need* large homes because we own so many things? Could we live with a lot less and share more? We need to see ourselves as who we really are; God does. We have not loved others as ourselves. We have loved ourselves.

The focal point of this parable seems to be that we should not be so concerned for material things that we ignore the more important spiritual things. It is an evangelistic message in a nutshell. But I wonder if it is too easily dismissed as just that by those of us whose souls are saved already? Could there be a message in it for us too? Do we ever depend on ourselves? Are we too caught up in material things? Do we ever feel that we have it made—that we can relax now—our insurance is paid up? Is there something of the rich man in us that we'd like to deny or forget? Is there covetousness lurking in a dark room somewhere within us?

We're all familiar with the Sermon on the Mount injunction: "Do not lay up for yourselves treasures on earth, where moth and rust consume and where thieves break in and steal. . . . For where your treasure is, there will your heart be also" (Matt. 6:19-21). Do we as Christians need to regularly evaluate the amount of earthly treasures we are accumulating? Is it possible that we ever deceive ourselves about where our treasure really is?

Second, I am concerned that affluent Christians (or not so affluent, covetousness is not limited to the rich) perceive that *they "need" so much* that there is little left to share with others. "He who loves money will not be satisfied with money; nor he who loves wealth, with gain; this also is vanity" (Eccl. 5:10).

We live in a society that says, "If you want it, get it." Television commercials say, "You deserve it." What's wrong with that? some might ask. Does anyone have the right to revel in plenty while one's neighbors grovel in poverty? I'm not so sure.

Mostly, I wonder about the kind of god we worship if we prepare our food in a microwave while others have no food. What kind of morality is this? Is the God that we worship unjust and unloving or is there something wrong with us?

A Christian must use moral judgment in determining what is enough for his personal needs. "There is a grievous evil which I have seen under the sun: riches were kept by their owner to his hurt. . . . He toiled for the wind, and spent all his days in darkness and grief, in much vexation and sickness and resentment" (Eccl. 5:13,16-17).

James Weaver, the American economist, suggests that our growth economy has its foundations in the assumption that man's wants are insatiable. Are Christians a part of this?

Third, I am concerned that we might *accept our*

blessings as a right and feel no compulsion to share our wealth with others in any significant way. Tradition taught that wealth was an indication of God's favor. The Book of Job clearly shows that tragedy and loss of wealth are not necessarily results of sin in a person's life, and the opposite is also true, wealth is not necessarily a sign of God's favor. The tradition lingered on, though, even in the time of Jesus. When Jesus said it is harder for a rich person to enter the kingdom of God than a camel to go through the eye of a needle, the disciples were shocked because riches were thought to represent God smiling down on a person's life.

Do we accept our affluence as a right because we are children of God? Do we expect it as a right because we are Americans? John Oliver Wilson, in his book, *After Affluence,* claims that the American dream has eroded. He defines the American dream in its many parts—educational advancement, a good job, upward mobility, a house in the suburbs, material abundance, and secure retirement. Is it possible that we Americans have put too much emphasis on the American dream and not enough emphasis on our Lord's warning in Matthew 6 to seek his kingdom first and allow him to meet our needs?

Fourth, I am concerned that we might fool ourselves into thinking that the Old Testament requirement of *one tenth is enough.* The tithe has traditionally been the gift of worship since time began, and the tithe is still the right gift for many. However, we live in a society in which many of us Christians have much more than we need. And so, we need to ask ourselves the question, "Is the tithe enough for me to give?"

Jesus doesn't say much about the tithe although he does mention it in passing to the Pharisees in Matthew 23:23. Paul calls on Christians to give in direct proportion to what they have been given. Each person must decide for himself. "Every one to whom much is given, of him will much be required" (Luke 12:48*b*).

> Giving is living, the angel said,
> Go feed to the hungry sweet charity's bread,
> And must I keep giving again and again?
> My selfish and querulous anger ran.
> Oh no! said the angel, piercing me through;
> Just give 'til the Master stops giving to you!
> —Author Unknown

Finally, I am concerned that in our independent, every-man-for-himself society, we will *forget, ignore, not notice the less fortunate people* of our communities and of our world.

God's will transforms economic relationships among his people. We see this in the early church (Acts 2:44-47). Christian philosopher Aristides, writing in AD 125 commented about the unique concern and sharing of this group of people held together with the bond of Christ.

The one who gave us this wonderful gift of prosperity has asked us to share it with our brothers and sisters. A. L. Palmer explained it this way, "Our sin in regard to wealth may be in keeping it when we ought to be giving it."[6]

One of the best examples of our need to share with others is one that Jesus gave Himself in Matthew 25:-31-45. It is not enough that Jesus is our Savior. Clearly, we are to serve him by serving others. In our age of self-gratification, we may need to reevaluate our service record.

I like the way Ronald Sider says it in his book, *Living More Simply:*

> In one way or another, the culture we live in is pushing us toward more elaborate living. No society in history has been so incessantly stimulated as ours to spend more and more money on nonessentials. And if the resulting materialism hinders our witness to a needy world, as it surely does, all the fault by no means lies with Madison Avenue and its unremitting appeals to self-indulgence. It also lies with us.[7]

---

1. "My World Is Hungry . . . Will I Care?" Christian Life Commission (Nashville: Convention Press, 1983.)
2. John V. Taylor, *Enough Is Enough* (Minneapolis: Augsburg Publishing House, 1977), p. 66.
3. *World Almanac and Book of Facts for 1983* (New York: World-Telegram, 1983).
4. "Issues and Answers: Hunger," Christian Life Commission (Nashville: Convention Press, 1983.)
5. James C. Dobson, "What Wives Wish Their Husbands Knew About Women," *Focus on the Family* film series, no. 7 (Waco, Texas: Educational Products Division, WORD, Inc., 1979.)

6. A. L. Palmer, *Stewardship Scripture Studies,* Vol. 3 (Nashville: n.p., 1971), p. 1.

7. Ronald J. Sider, *Living More Simply: Biblical Principles and Practical Models* (Downers Grove, Ill.: Intervarsity Press, 1980), p. 28.

The World in the Local Church

In our day when "acceptable" worship is so closely related to dress—education—culture—buildings and equipment, the non-essentials often take precedence over that which is vital.

—H. B. Ramsour

We have looked at materialism in ourselves as individual Christians. Our churches are but extensions of ourselves. If material things are highly valued by the individuals who make up the local congregations, those same values will show up in the decisions of those churches.

Look with me for a moment with your mind's eye at the building in which your church meets. How much of what is there is really essential to spreading the gospel? Are there pews, carpet, draperies, organ, piano, fellowship hall, modern kitchen, air conditioning, stained-glass windows, a lovely sanctuary, and much more? What about the building itself? Is it large enough? Is it attractive enough?

A friend recently told me that he had always felt that our church buildings should be as nicely appointed as our own homes with carpet, fine furniture, and so on. After all, we should be willing to spend as freely for the Lord as we do for ourselves. Then his point of view changed. Is that really what God wants: fine pews and carpet? Now instead of championing equal rights for our church buildings, he wonders why our homes need all of these comfortable extras. In essence, we need to be good stewards of what God has given in our homes and in our church buildings.

Just a careful look at a typical church budget will show where most of our gifts for the kingdom go, and, in so doing, it will give us an idea about the values of the church people who made the budget. Look at your own church budget. What proportion is spent on debt reduction, the physical plant, maintenance, utilities, and so on? How much is spent strictly for evangelism and benevolence? We can't tell, you say. We can't divide it like that; we have to have heat, light, and a building to meet in or we can't have evangelism or benevolence. Heat and debt retirement are money guzzlers that eat up a valuable proportion of our church budgets. They are essential because we have made traditional church buildings and their trappings essential to the gospel ministry. It's possible that all the things that we think are essential are not as necessary as we thought. We may need to consider some alternatives in order to be better stewards of our tithes and offerings.

What are the essentials of a New Testament church? Look at Acts 4:31-35 for some clarification.

> And when they had prayed, the place in which they were gathered together was shaken; and they were all filled with the Holy Spirit and spoke the word of God with boldness. Now the company of

> those who believed were of one heart and soul, and no one said that any of the things which he possessed was his own, but they had everything in common. And with great power the apostles gave their testimony to the resurrection of the Lord Jesus, and great grace was upon them all. There was not a needy person among them, for as many as were possessors of lands or houses sold them, and brought the proceeds of what was sold and laid it at the apostles' feet; and distribution was made to each as any had need.

What was a New Testament church like? Did it have a fine building? An organ? Beautiful cushioned pews? Carpet? A cathedral ceiling? A large educational building? A fellowship hall? A modern kitchen? Air conditioning? I doubt it.

What were the essentials that it did have? Look again at the passage. The church had an *active prayer life.* It had the *Holy Spirit.* It had *boldness.* It had *unity.* It had *sharing.* It had *power.* It had *testimony.*

But some will inevitably say, "But if we're really going to grow, we need an adequate facility, and a beautiful sanctuary for all the people we hope to reach for God." Was the New Testament church growing? Read Acts 2:41 and 5:14. It was growing by leaps and bounds. Why? It had the essential qualities for growth. What churches need to grow is not always reflected in the church budget.

Waldo J. Werning warns, "The secularistic and

materialistic motives of our society have invaded the church, many of them contradicting the Gospel plan."[2]

Have we carried our materialism into our churches? Are we too hung up on our buildings to do any real good?

> In the first century, church referred to a group of people, rather than a building as we so often use the term today. Christians did not begin to build church buildings until about A.D. 200. This fact suggests that, whatever else church buildings are good for, they are not essential either for numerical growth or spiritual depth. The early church possessed both these qualities, and the church's greatest period of growth and vitality until recent times was during the first two centuries A.D. In other words, the church grew fastest when it did not have the help—or hindrance—of church buildings.[3]

Arbutus B. Sider, a contributor to *Living More Simply* reminds us,

> We know that the Lord is present in his people, not the building. We know that simplicity does not preclude beauty, and we know that worship is not a time to escape from the ugliness of the world around us. Rather, worship is a time to bring the needs of the world into the beauty of his holiness. The Lord is present in his sanctuary, no matter how humble it may be.[4]

"But if it is really true that church buildings are not essential either for growth or spirituality, why do churches today depend so heavily on buildings? Is it true the church suffers an 'edifice complex'?" Howard Snyder asks.

The gospel is always new and produces change; that's what Jesus meant about new wine. But structures become rigid with time like old wineskins. So we can't put new wine in old wineskins. We need to be always renewing our structures which carry the gospel, to keep them doing what they were originally created to do—spread the kingdom and build up the church. According to Howard Snyder, "We end up serving the structure instead of the structure serving the church."[5]

It may be that traditional church buildings have outlived their usefulness, as functional as they might be. When we consider how much money we invest in them in the face of problems of energy and world hunger, it might be good stewardship to consider some alternatives. We could consider meeting in homes, community centers, multipurpose buildings, or share church buildings on a cooperative basis. Good suggestions for alternative meeting places are provided in *Living More with Less* by Doris Longacre and *Living More Simply: Biblical Principles and Practical Models* by Ronald J. Sider.

Let me share an illustration of a viable alternative to building a church building that means many long years of debt retirement and high interest payments. About eight years ago, when Doug Pilot came to pastor Greencastle Baptist Church, the people were meeting in an old Pennsylvania Railroad station. He felt a strong conviction that the church, then only about thirty-five members, should try to build a facility without borrowing money from a bank. At first, the small church thought that he was crazy. Pilot was not shaken. He believed that if they trusted in the Lord, He would provide. His conviction was based on Philippians 4:19: "And my God will supply every need of yours according to his riches in glory in Christ Jesus."

One year later, the chairman of the deacons shared with the congregation on a Sunday morning that he and his family had been praying about taking this very same step of faith, and that they wanted to commit themselves publicly to building without borrowing. Most of the rest of the membership stood to show that they agreed.

Some asked, "How will we achieve this—with bake sales and car washes?" The pastor answered emphatically, "No, we'll trust the Lord." From then on, Philippians 4:19 became their watchword. The church was committed.

They later purchased property where the church is now located, using their savings accounts. The man who sold them the property only wanted one half of the money that first year so that they could draw interest on the other half to be used for building materials.

In the next few years an interesting thing happened. Although the general funds never came up short, the building fund began to grow greatly, more than $1,000 a month. They bought materials as money was available, and money became available as materials were needed.

The people could see God's hand working in the midst of them: touching the hearts of people and providing each time a need arose. This went on for three years until the church was built. The church members did all the work themselves with the exception of two tasks, one of which was pouring the concrete floor. But members assisted there, too. Three men even took a class at the local vocational-technical center in order to lead the others in laying brick.

Many people outside the church also volunteered their time, services, and equipment without being asked, to assist in this exciting challenge that God's people had taken on. There were also many cash gifts from friends of the church.

Every step of the way, the Lord provided what was needed at that moment. Finally, some important decisions needed to be made about where to go from here. The church had a day of prayer and fasting to seek the Lord's direction concerning these financial matters (Jehoshaphat, 2 Chron. 20:3). God answered in a mighty way with a $3,000 gift from an old friend of the pastor, just at the time they needed it.

Their facility cost them about one third of what they might have spent building it the traditional way. The money they saved can be used for missions and meeting human needs. This isn't to say that all churches should take this route in building facilities. Not all of us would be willing or able to commit ourselves to the time, energy, and giving that is required in a project like this. But it is an exciting alternative to those who will claim His promise to supply our needs. It is also an unshakable testimony to what God will do for any people who desire to glorify Him in that way.

We might need to rethink our goals. We want to see people saved and disciples nurtured, but that doesn't necessitate large churches. It could mean planting many small ones. We could copy one of our methods for growing in Sunday School classes, which is *divide and multiply.* When a class reaches a certain size, for example, ten or twelve, we often divide it into two smaller classes. Then each of those two smaller classes reaches out to others and grows. Then, when the time comes, they divide again. Churches could use this formula more often, but instead, many churches continue to grow larger and larger, requiring more space and building programs, and, often lose the close sharing and fellowship they once enjoyed. The building programs which devour funds could be used more directly for evangelism and benevolence. Smaller churches could then meet in large homes or rented space. Churches would become known for who they are and what they do in Christ's name rather than where they meet. Our churches would become more like New Testament churches. I wonder if we could stand it? But I doubt that we'll ever do it. Christianity in America seems to prefer the "old wineskins."

Tony Campolo, in his film, *It's Friday, but Sunday's Comin'* gives us this warning,

> With 500,000,000 people in the world suffering from malnutrition, the church has to ask itself some questions. We have $180 billion wrapped up in buildings. What does the Lord have to say to a church that has $180 billion in buildings while children die because they don't have their basic needs met. All of these buildings were built to honor somebody who said, "I dwell not in temples made with hands" (Acts 7:48). (Acts 17:24 makes essentially the same point.) It's about time that we as the church get our priorities straightened out. Jesus called us to bring good news to the poor, the oppressed and the suffering peoples of the world. And that means that we're going to have to get off our affluent kick and recognize that God calls us not to be rich, but to give it away to those who are downtrodden.[6]

If we gave less emphasis to our buildings and the long list of needs that follow after them, what a wealth of money would be freed for people needs and evangelism! Think about it.

I worry about the priorities of our churches when we can raise thousands of dollars in a campaign to get an organ or some other expensive equipment, but we can only raise a few hundred dollars for foreign missions or world hunger. The logic that we can't afford to give more does not hold water. Waldo J. Werning in his book, *The Stewardship Call,* claims that the church develops a type of "sanctified materialism," a kind of materialism that is acceptable to us because of the "higher purposes" that we bestow on it.

Let us not forget that the purpose of our stewardship is not the survival of the institutional church. In teaching His people to give, God did not stress the needs of the Temple or of the Levites. He urged people to give in gratitude for the abundance He had given them.

Doris Longacre, author of *Living More with Less,* says, "Our church buildings may or may not impress God, but they make an indelible impression on visitors from underdeveloped countries."[7] When Christians, who are natives of underdeveloped countries, visit in America and see that the cost of one of our church buildings could provide four or more "churches" in their own country, they have reason to be concerned about the priorities of North American Christians.

OK, you say, what if we already have a large, expensive building in which to meet? What can we do? We can find new ways to use it to serve God and others in addition to worship and meetings. What are some of the possibilities?

The church can open the doors of its meeting place to provide space for Bible release time, if there is such a program in your community.

It can provide a facility for wholesome community endeavors and youth activities such as scouting. It can sponsor its own youth activities to provide wholesome leisuretime activities and contact with the Christian community.

The open church can provide day care or preschool

activities, services that are much in demand now. Much thought and planning (as well as a license, possibly) are required to make this ministry succeed, but the opportunities and rewards can be great.

The church can use its building for a food pantry or secondhand clothing warehouse to serve community and churchwide needs. In this case, you will want to coordinate your plans with other community and church groups to avoid duplicating efforts.

With the support of a nucleus of skilled church members, establish a fix-it shop to minister to elderly or disadvantaged in your community.

There are so many possibilities, but we need to put on our creative thinking caps and find the ones that are right for our church and our community.

We can let the world know that a church is not just a group of self-righteous people who meet two or three times a week to sing and pray, but that the church is a group of sinners who have been saved and changed by the blood of the Lamb, and who care because He cared.

Whenever the Israelites lived closely with pagan cultures, they slowly began to assimilate the foreign practices, even to the point of worshiping pagan gods. God's prophets were constantly calling them back from their unfaithfulness. One of the gods of this culture is things. To a great extent, our local churches have assimilated this American culture, which, in a sense, is pagan also, and made it part of our own. We have seriously strayed from our New Testament model, and stand in desperate need of God's prophet to call us back.

---

1. B. Ramsour, *Stewardship Scripture Studies,* Vol. 3 (Nashville: n.p., 1971), p. 89.

2. Waldo J. Werning, *The Stewardship Call* (St. Louis: Concordia Publishing House, 1962), p. 45.

3. Howard A. Snyder, *The Problem of Wineskins: Church Structure in a Technological Age* (Downers Grove, Ill.: Intervarsity Press, 1975), p. 69.

4. Arbutus B. Sider, *Living More Simply: Biblical Principles and Practical Models* (Downers Grove, Ill.: Intervarsity Press, 1980), p. 126.

5. Snyder, p. 69.

6. Anthony Campolo, *It's Friday, but Sunday's Comin'* (Waco, Texas: WORD, Inc., 1982). Used by permission.

7. Doris Longacre, *Living More with Less* (Scottsdale, Pa.: Herald Press, 1980), p. 231.

It's Not Ours, Anyway!

The earth is the Lord's and the fullness thereof, the world and those who dwell therein (Ps. 24:1).

We don't like to hear about giving. It's too personal; it comes too close to where we live. The pastor can preach on almost any other subject and we'll listen, but let him preach on stewardship and we'll likely tune him out.

Every year as church budgets are being prepared, there is a great tendency among pastors to preach stewardship sermons. There are also tithing testimonies, witnessing to what God has done in the lives of those who have consented to tithe. I had occasion to visit a church of another denomination while traveling one weekend. On that particular Sunday the pastor preached a wonderful and stimulating sermon on stewardship with the primary emphasis on giving. As soon as it was over, one of the church members apologized to me. What a shame I had come to visit only to hear a sermon about giving! As if to say, "Our pastor does better than that most of the time; sorry, he slipped up today."

Many of us have a poor attitude about the role of

giving in our Christian lives. W. L. Muncy Jr., reflects, "Stewardship is as comprehensive as the life of the believer, and it is not something that the Christian may put on like a garment, may practice, if he cares to do so; but that it is what he must be and do, if he is to be genuinely Christian. It is just that basic, comprehensive and significant."[1]

We Christians somehow start on the wrong foot when we get the idea through our church's teaching or annual stewardship campaigns that we've made it if we tithe. We think we can spend the other nine tenths on ourselves and our families as we see fit. Stewardship doesn't work that way. Everything we have and are belongs to God.

"For all things come from thee, and of thine own we have given thee. O Lord our God, all this abundance that we have provided for building thee a house for thy holy name comes from thy hand and is all thy own" (1 Chron. 29:14*b*,16).

"The land shall not be sold in perpetuity, for the land is mine; for you are strangers and sojourners with me" (Lev. 25:23). The material world ultimately and finally belongs to God. "For all the earth is mine" (Ex. 19:5*c*).

"The Biblical principle of the relation of humanity to God's world is not ownership but stewardship. We who live in the most wasteful society in the world, which is consuming God-given resources at an unparalleled rate, must take that perspective seriously."[2]

We are not owners, but stewards. "Steward" comes from the Greek word *oikonomos*. It is a compound noun referring to household management. "Christian stewardship is a family affair, God's children working with him, sharing his purpose, resources, and very nature."[3]

Waldo Werning in *The Stewardship Call* gives this definition:

> Christian stewardship is the believer's response to God's love in creating, preserving, redeeming, and sanctifying him. It can be called the Christian's management of his redeemed life and possessions, by the Spirit's power and direction through the word—to God's glory and for man's benefit. Christian stewardship is the fruit of saving faith. It is faith in action, the expression of Christian faith, the evidence of how sincerely the child of God believes the truths he embraces. A Christian steward is a person who is entrusted with a life redeemed by Christ. To be a steward is to follow where God leads by the abilities and the strength He gives.[4]

Christian stewardship is neither a department of life nor a sphere of activity but a conception of life as a whole displayed in attitudes and action. The practice of Christian stewardship should be the joyful overflow of gratitude as an expression of one's personal fellowship with one's Lord. It is a response to God, not a bargaining for His favor.

Some think of stewardship as a whip or a legal action to drive people to give to the expenses of the

> church. No doubt too often the attempt has been made to wring generous offerings from selfish souls. Christian stewardship most certainly is not church legislation nor a scheme to deprive men of their cash. It is the natural consequence of an experience with God—the natural reaction of the human heart that has been touched by the divine Spirit.[5]

Even though man has "messed up" an otherwise good creation, he is still entrusted with things which were created by and owned by God. Out of His abundant supply, God provides for every need. We are accountable to Him.

Stewardship is the opposite of covetousness. Covetousness begins when we stop believing God. God cares for man, yet man continues to worry and fret for himself because he cannot fully believe that God knows what He's doing. Worry is man's silent way of saying that he can't trust God; he must take on the job himself.

As I look at America, I am reminded of the Lord's words to Israel as the people prepared to go into the Promised Land.

> For the Lord your God is bringing you into a good land, a land of brooks of water, of fountains and springs, flowing forth in valleys and hills, a land of wheat and barley, of vines and fig trees and pomegranates, a land of olive trees and honey, a land in which you will eat bread without scarcity,

> in which you will lack nothing, a land whose stones are iron, and out of whose hills you can dig copper. And you shall eat and be full, and you shall bless the Lord your God for the good land he has given you (Deut. 8:7-14).
>
> Take heed lest you forget the Lord your God, by not keeping his commandments and his ordinances and his statutes, which I command you this day: lest, when you have eaten and are full, and have built goodly houses and live in them, and when your herds and flocks multiply, and your silver and gold is multiplied, and all that you have is multiplied, then your heart be lifted up, and you forget the Lord your God, who brought you out of the land of Egypt, out of the house of bondage. Beware lest you say in your heart, "My power and the might of my hand have gotten me this wealth." You shall remember the Lord your God, for it is he who gives you power to get wealth (vv. 17-18*a*).

Can you see America in this passage? Our country was founded by a group of people seeking a place to raise their families and worship God as they felt led. Life was hard for the first colonists as it was for the Israelites who wandered in the desert for forty years because of their disobedience. In the last few decades, life has become good, very good, for the majority of Americans. And when life is good, we tend to forget the source.

When we forget the source of our abilities and wealth

and take the credit for ourselves, we lose our main motivation for unselfish giving. We begin to tell ourselves, "I earned it; it's mine."

God warned His people then about this dangerous attitude. I expect He's trying to warn us today. Humanity hasn't changed very much.

I can hear someone asking, "Well, how much are we to give? Isn't the tithe the rule for Christians, too?" Since there is very little in the New Testament about the tithe, I began to wonder about the origin of this tradition of Christian giving. Is the tenth what God expects of us as new creatures? Or is there a new law for those who would call themselves followers of Christ?

The origin of the tenth being the acceptable rate for paying tribute to rulers and as offerings or religious gifts is not completely known. The tithe existed in Babylon, Persia, Egypt, and even in China in ancient times. Hebrews 7:4 indicates that the tithe was the accepted offering in Abraham's day also. It was a widespread custom to divide the spoils of war with rulers and religious leaders. Jacob's covenant with God at Bethel included payment of tithes.

Customs in paying the tithe varied since definite legal requirements were long in coming. At first the tither was to share his tithe with the Levites (Deut. 14:22-23).

"The methods developed for paying the tithes and for their use became somewhat complicated, when to the tithe of the first fruits were added the firstlings of the flocks."[6]

Tithes were paid for the upkeep of the sons of Levi when the Levitical system was established. The Temple was the place to which the tithe was taken.

Each Hebrew was to make an announcement establishing his own honesty before the Lord in order to avoid deceitful tithing practices (Deut. 26:13-15).

In New Testament times it was increasingly difficult for people to tithe because of the poor economic life in Judea under Roman rule. However, the New Testament does not teach a lower standard for giving than the law. The fact that the Pharisees tithed even the herbs used for seasoning was evidence that the law of the tenth was still observed. Jesus always poured deeper meaning into the law. In Matthew 23:23 Jesus rebukes the Pharisees for giving the tithe, but neglecting "the weightier matters of the law, justice and mercy and faith." Tithing is good, but they were missing the joy that comes from responding in justice, mercy, faith, and compassion.

Waldo Werning explains:

> The Gospel, not the Law, furnishes the motive power for Christian stewardship. While the Law only causes the Christian to pull his cloak of stubborn resistance and unwillingness more closely about himself, the sun of the Gospel with its penetrating power and warming love induces and en-

> ables the steward to pull off his cloak of selfishness and to get to work in the service of his Lord.[7]

The standard since the coming of Jesus seems to be giving in proportion, giving "according to his ability" (Acts 11:29), giving "as he may prosper" (1 Cor. 16:2), and giving "according to their means" (2 Cor. 8:3). This means that some would be giving a tenth while some might be giving much more.

According to Werning,

> The tithe is not man's real problem. His real problem lies in putting God first and giving generously. Most people have real spiritual problems and attitudes to change and conquer first before they can think about tithing.[8]

A majority of Christians in North America today are not like the poor fishermen of the first-century church. We are affluent. To people in emerging nations, we are affluent beyond their wildest dreams. We may not feel rich, but, compared to those in extreme poverty, we are. It's true that not all Christians have been blessed in such a great way materially. But for those of us who have, what responsibility comes with it?

We cannot separate stewardship from its social implications. Sitting in our pews on Sunday and bringing our tithes regularly cannot be a substitute for responding to human needs in our community and world. Tithing does not excuse our ignoring people's needs. A fair share of a tithe is recycled back into our own church, which, in case we hadn't noticed, meets some of our own needs.

We gladly give our tenth to the Lord's work, but what about *the other nine tenths?* Even if we're not trying to keep up with the Joneses, do we selfishly spend it on ourselves? Do we forget that it all belongs to God? Do we shut our eyes to the vast needs of others even though we claim to love them in Jesus' name? Can we distinguish between our *needs* and our *wants?* Do we who have been called after His name have the compassion of Christ? Have we asked our Lord to free us from our love of money? And finally, are we doing something with our compassion? Are we using the whole ten tenths to glorify God in this world?

---

1. W. L. Muncy, Jr., *Fellowship with God Through Christian Stewardship* (Kansas City, Mo.: Kansas City Central Seminary Press).
2. Ronald Sider, p. 31.
3. John Alexander, *Stewardship Scripture Studies,* Vol. 5 (Nashville: n.p., 1983), pp. 7-8.
4. Werning, p. 18.
5. Milo Kauffman, *The Challenge of Christian Stewardship* (Scottsdale, Pa.: Herald Press, 1955), p. 5.
6. From *Zondervan Pictorial Bible Dictionary,* Merrill G. Tenney, ed., 1963.
7. Werning, pp. 55-56.
8. Werning, p. 90.

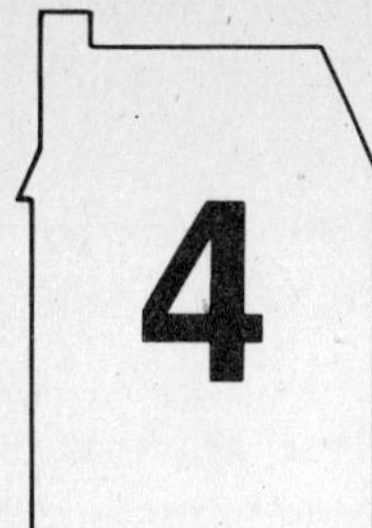

Why Give?

He has showed you, O man, what is good;
and what does the Lord require of you
but to do justice, and to love kindness,
and to walk humbly with your God?
(Mic. 6:8).

There are many valid reasons for generous giving which can be supported by Scripture. Our motives for giving as Christians are, most likely, a composite of several of these reasons. You may think of others as you consider these.

We give generously to spread the gospel of Jesus Christ throughout the world. We give to support the preaching ministry of our local church and missions efforts worldwide, because that is what we are about.

We give generously because we are stewards of what God has given us. We recognize that all we have is from God; on that basis, we cannot hoard money or possessions because we are not the ultimate owners, rather, we are stewards (1 Chron. 29:14*b*). As stewards, we want to imitate God's generous nature by unselfish giving to Him and others.

We give generously because we want to identify with the poor as God did. Throughout Scripture, both in the Old and New Testaments, our Lord champions the cause of the poor. That is not to say that He is not concerned about all people, but we could say that the Lord empathizes with the "underdog": the poor, the abused, the powerless. He gave up the riches of heaven to come to a spiritual wilderness to bring mankind into relationship with Him.

We give generously because giving leads to spiritual growth. Giving is good for us as people. It has been said that God doesn't need our gifts as much as we need to give.

We give generously in response to love. We want to be obedient to our Creator and Savior. Jesus said, "If you love me, you will keep my commandments" (John 14:15). Obedience is always an appropriate test of and response to love. We parents know that the words "Mommy (or Daddy), I love you," would seem shallow in the face of continual disobedience. Our Father, who has urged us to love and to give freely, must feel great disappointment when we fail to obey and keep much of our material blessings for ourselves.

We give generously because it is the natural result of loving our neighbors as ourselves. We are always eager to meet our own needs. If we love others with *agape* love as God intended, we will be concerned enough to help others meet their needs to the extent that we are able. We may be able to help more than we think if we can let go of some of our luxuries to meet the basic needs of our neighbors. It could be that we need to live more simply so that others can simply live.

We give generously to respond to overwhelming needs. We are constantly learning about the needs faced by our home and foreign missionaries: medical supplies, worship facilities, literature, food, money for salaries to keep our missionaries in the field. We see the needs of our own church budgets which allow us to keep our doors open so that we can continue proclaiming the Word. We see the needs in our communities: the unemployed, the refugees, those caught in the welfare treadmill, the untrained, and the elderly poor. We see the needs in our world where few have much and many have little. It seems like a mission impossible, but we must give where we see need, knowing that Jesus did.

We give generously to avoid covetousness and greed. "All day long the wicked covets, but the righteous gives and does not hold back" (Prov. 21:26). Jesus often warned those who had been blessed materially about the negative effect that wealth can have in a person's life (Mark 10:23,25; Luke 12:15,29-31). The good life can lead to trusting self and a life of greed. Giving freely of what God has given us will help us to avoid that pitfall.

We give generously, knowing we will be happier if we do. "Remembering the words of the Lord Jesus, how he said, 'It is more blessed to give than to receive' " (Acts 20:35*b*). By "blessed," Jesus did not mean we will be holier if we give, but happier. Hopefully, this is not our sole purpose for giving, but rather, it is one of the fruits of generous giving that God bestows on the giver. In giving freely we find joy, and that joy is one motivation for further giving.

We give generously because it is a wise investment. "He who gives to the poor will not want,/but he who hides his eyes will get many a curse" (Prov. 28:27). We live in an uncertain world. We are all concerned about providing for our future, having security in our old age. Jesus says one's best investment is using one's money to serve Him rather than oneself (Matt. 6:19-20).

Many of us tithe through our churches. That's one reason it is wise to be involved in budget planning and not be ignorant of what our tithes are used for. In most churches the undesignated gift goes for staff salaries, missions, utilities, literature, building maintenance, debt retirement and interest, office supplies, educational programs, benevolence, and so forth. Each church varies, to some extent, in the way it uses its gifts.

One of the best ways to further God's kingdom through our giving is to give freely through our churches in which the gospel is preached regularly. It is easy, however, to make the tithe to our church the *limit* of our giving. The tithe should be a minimum figure—not a maximum figure. In a world in which many of us have so much more than we need, we are able to increase the standard of our giving as we have increased our standard of living.

I am concerned not only that we have neglected giving through our churches but also that our giving has stopped at the church door. If we give to our church, are we then free to ignore the needs around us?

Do we want to help our neighbor who has lost his job? Do we offer confidential assistance to the church friend who is experiencing rough times? Are we available to the young woman who is rearing her children alone?

Do we seek out those in the community who could benefit from our help? Are we sensitive to the vast needs of the world to hear the gospel and have the basic necessities of life? Are we concerned enough to give to meet these needs over and above our tithe? Do we assume a tenth is enough, and then allow ourselves to live in excess with the other nine tenths? Do we allow the importance of spiritual needs over physical needs to be an excuse for not giving when we see basic needs for food, clothing, and shelter going unmet? Is our giving a form of tokenism or do we really care enough to give generously?

The truth is that we Christians don't necessarily give generously. Sometimes I think we fool ourselves. Many times we make excuses for our giving, or not giving, just as those who were invited to the great banquet (Luke 14:16-24) made excuses for why they couldn't come to the Lord's banquet. I'm sure our Lord sees our excuses for what they are just as He did when He told that parable.

Let us look at some of the excuses that we make. Check the ones that you might have used before.

______ 1. I don't give much because I don't like the way our church spends its money.

______ 2. Our church has a big budget; it doesn't need my money.

______ 3. If they (the poor) were willing to work for a living like I do, they wouldn't need my help.

______ 4. The organization just used the money I sent

to them to send more people letters asking for contributions.

______ 5. Why should I send money overseas for the poor when there are poor people here in my country?

______ 6. Things are bad economically everywhere now; I'm having to tighten my belt, too.

______ 7. I am helping them; who do you think pays for their welfare checks?

______ 8. Jesus said it himself; there will always be poor people.

______ 9. What I can give seems only a drop in the bucket. What difference will it make to a world of poverty?

______10. I tithe—that's enough, isn't it?

______11. God helps them who helps themselves. That's my philosophy.

______12. Am I my brother's keeper?

______13. Everybody in my family is working.

______14. You have to be careful who you give to. Some people just don't deserve it. They'll take advantage of you if they can.

______15. Christians are to be good stewards of their money; therefore we should not give too liberally to those who may misuse our gift.

Why are these just excuses? Allow me to respond.

1. If this is a real concern to you, get involved in the budget planning of your church. Discuss your concerns with other members if you don't feel your church is setting the right priorities. Others might agree with you. Don't simply withhold your money.

2. Don't be deterred from your giving by a healthy

church budget. Challenge yourself to find a new ministry that your church can take on in which your offerings can help. Or challenge your church to give more to missions.

3. This is an oversimplification. For many people in our society, jobs and skills which are needed to acquire them are hard to obtain, especially in times of recession. In other parts of the world, there are additional problems. Wages are extremely low, and needed goods are scarce. Most of us would fare no better in our brother's shoes.

4. *Yes,* it is wise to check into how your gift money is being spent. Naturally, some human service organizations are more efficient at getting the money to the needy than others. By all means, do check it out. *No,* it is not a good reason for not giving to world hunger. We are so cautious. (With the size of some of our gifts, I'm sure these organizations need to solicit a great deal more.)

5. This is the old "bait and switch" tactic. It works fine as long as nobody asks you how much you are doing to help the needy in your country, community, or church. Glad you noticed—there are needs right here, too!

6. This is probably true, but most of us middle-class Christians don't have any idea what it's like to be really poor. We think we're hungry if dinner is a little late. Others are literally starving to death. To the truly poor, we are rich.

7. Yes, we are helping (if you can call it that) in a small way by paying our share of involuntary taxes. Even the heathen do that much.

8. Yes, he did, and, taken out of context that is enough for those who are looking for an excuse not to give. The fact that there will always be poor is no reason for not meeting the needs as we see them. God commands that we do so.

9. What you can give will make a big difference to someone who is cold or hungry. It will meet those needs temporarily and say to the person(s), "I care."

10. No, it's not. The tithe is an Old Testament minimal guideline. We are the New Testament church. Love is our guideline. Without it, legalism rears its ugly head.

11. Many poor people are doing the best they can, and it is still not enough. Besides, who made us the judges? We are the instruments of God's love. Are we properly tuned?

12. You guessed it. Jesus was our example, making the ultimate sacrifice to meet human need.

13. If you shut your eyes and don't truly see, you don't feel the responsibility for responding to need. But the needs don't go away because we don't see them, and neither does our responsibility (Matt. 9:36).

14. Once again, we are judging. We are deciding who is worthy of our gifts. I am glad that God didn't use our measuring stick when He decided to bless us. We are sinners, too. Our part is to give as God has given to us. Leave the rest to God.

15. Mark Galli, in his article entitled, "Five Reasons for Not Giving to the Poor,"[1] suggests that this is a weak rationale for not giving because; (1) the poor are not necessarily less responsible with money and possessions than we are, (2) many of us learned to be respon-

sible with money the hard way, by having an allowance and wasting it, (3) the teachings of Jesus contradict this "good stewardship" rationale, (4) some abuse is inevitable (Luke 17:11-19), and (5) if more should not be given to those who are wasteful, then God should withdraw His bountiful blessings from us.

When we have more money than we need, which is often a reality in affluent nations whether we admit it or not, we have but two choices. We can spend it on ourselves or we can give it away.

---

1. Mark Galli, "Five Reasons for Not Giving to the Poor," *Christianity Today* (November 25, 1983), pp. 28-29.

5 If You Really Loved Me . . .

A new commandment I give to you, that you love one another; even as I have loved you, that you also love one another. By this all men will know that you are my disciples, if you have love for one another (John 13:34-35).

• My name is Loki. I live in Thailand. I am thirteen. There are six people in our family. We farm a small piece of land. Our family income is about $600 a year. There is little money; life is hard. My father says that in a few years I will have to go to the city to get a job. This little scrap of land will not support us all when we grow up. I don't want to leave my family, but I think I must do like other young men are doing. My parents love us. They want to give us a better life, but they cannot. It hurts them, I know.

• My name is Sarah Hill. I live in Philadelphia (The City of Brotherly Love). I am seventy-six years old. I live alone. My husband died ten years ago. Sometimes I think it would have been better if I had gone then, too. I receive a check for $320 a month. It is hard to make ends meet. Everything is so expensive. It's difficult to make it now. Sometimes I am hungry, but there isn't much food in the refrigerator. When you are old, people just don't care about you anymore.

• My name is Rosa. I live in Mexico. I am eight. We

have seven in our family, including Grandma. She lives with us. We grow most of our own food. We own a cow; she gives milk. But there aren't many pesos left to buy the things we need. My mother and father say that Americans are rich. When they come to our country, they have fancy clothes and other things. Our friends and neighbors are all poor like we are, but we try to share if we can. Americans are our neighbors, but they don't share with us. What kind of neighbors are *they?*

A great theologian was once asked by a reporter what was the greatest theological truth of all time. The great man of theology studied and thought for a week before he replied. At the end of the week, he came back to the reporter and said, "After years of study and a week of meditation, the greatest theological truth that I know is 'God is love.' " God is still trying to communicate that truth to all the world and we are His messengers. I can't help wondering what kind of job we're doing with the Lokis and Sarahs and Rosas of this world.

As I began to research material for this book, I realized that a great deal has already been written on the subject of affluence and poverty in our world and the Christian's responsibility to it. So, in a way I felt that I had begun to rehash a subject about which much had already been written. No matter how much has been written in the past, it was clear to me that we Christians hadn't learned our lessons yet. Although I have a strong determination with God's help to change it, I must include myself in that *we.*

Although we've just considered many reasons for giving, of which meeting human need is only one, I am strongly convicted by the Holy Spirit that we need to stop fooling ourselves on this issue. We're certainly not fooling God. Either we care or we don't care. I'd like to think that Christians care.

It seems to me if we preach Christ and are willing to ignore the other basic human needs of our fellowman because of our own personal selfishness, we have lost touch with the scope of Jesus' ministry to the whole person.

Most of us who have come to know Christ in our comfortable home or comfortable sanctuary with healthy bodies, stomachs full, and decent clothing, can say to ourselves that none of these physical kinds of things really matters. And, in terms of eternity, that is true (see Lazarus, Luke 16:20-25). But that doesn't negate our responsibility to show God's love. I fear that we pass off hunger, disease, and other *preventable* life-and-death matters lightly because we never experience real hunger or have had a child who was brain damaged from lack of protein.

Of the many things that we could say about God's love, we could certainly say that it is unselfish. After all, God created this abundant world for us and was willing to sacrifice His own Son to bring us, His sinful people, back into relationship with Him.

This disparity between His *agape* love for people and

our convenient love for people is striking. I believe selfishness is at the core of the problem, and we don't see our own selfishness.

Gladys Hunt, a contributor to *Living More Simply,* reminds us,

> To be unconcerned that our rising affluence is crippling already poverty-stricken nations should be unthinkable. One-third of the world's population consumes three-fourths of the world's protein every year, and we are part of that one-third. A different third of the world's people has an annual per capita income of $100 or less. We cannot ignore the cry of hungry neighbors.[1]

With that in mind, I devote this chapter to world need and our Christian responsibility to meet rather than ignore it.

God Identifies with the Poor

Throughout His Word, God repeatedly identifies with the poor and downtrodden. He commands that we live in a loving relationship with others.

> Is this not the fast that I choose;
> to loose the bonds of wickedness,
> to undo the thongs of the yoke,
> to let the oppressed go free,
> and to break every yoke?
> Is it not to share your bread with the hungry,
> and bring the homeless poor into your house;

when you see the naked, to cover him,

....

and not to hide yourself from your own flesh?
if you pour yourself out for the hungry
and satisfy the desire of the afflicted,
then shall your light rise in the darkness
and your gloom be as the noonday" (Isa. 58:6-10).

There will always be a problem with poverty in the world, so why bother, some would say. God recognizes the persistence of poverty in this kind of world. He does not, however, tolerate a passive acceptance of poverty. "For the poor will never cease out of the land; therefore I command you, You shall open wide your hand to your brother, to the needy and to the poor, in the land" (Deut. 15:11). Notice that God doesn't come to us meekly asking His people to share their prosperity with a hungry world, He commands it. Are we not His people? Are we not prosperous? Is poverty no longer a problem in our world?

> For I was hungry and you gave me food, I was thirsty and you gave me drink, I was a stranger and you welcomed me, I was naked and you clothed me, I was sick and you visited me, I was in prison and you came to me. Then the righteous will answer him, "Lord, when did we see thee hungry and feed thee, or thirsty and give thee drink? And when did we see thee a stranger and welcome thee, or naked and clothe thee? And when did we

> see thee sick or in prison and visit thee?" And the King will answer them, "Truly, I say to you, as you did it to one of the least of these my brethren, you did it to me" (Matt. 25:35-40).

Again, our Lord was identifying Himself with the poor and suffering.

Jesus declared that His purpose for coming into the world was inherently connected to the poor and suffering of this world.

> The Spirit of the Lord is upon me,
> because he has anointed me to preach
> good news to the poor.
> He has sent me to proclaim release to the captives
> and recovering of sight to the blind
> to set at liberty those who are oppressed,
> to proclaim the acceptable year of the Lord
> (Luke 4:18-19).

Although the words *poor, captives,* and *blind* describe the spiritual bankruptcy to which the gospel of Jesus is directed, we cannot ignore the fact that Jesus did, indeed, identify with the poor, the afflicted, and the powerless. So these words cannot be interpreted only in the symbolic sense. Jesus ministered to the *total* person.

"He who is kind to the poor lends to the Lord" (Prov. 19:17). "I know that the Lord maintains the cause of the afflicted,/and executes justice for the needy" (Ps. 140:12).

> Genuine love does not ignore humanity in its great misery. True Christian love discovers and knows that the neighbor exists. To receive God's love is to be set aflame with that same love for the ministry or stewardship that He gave us. The function of the body is to make its members available to one another and to their Head, Jesus Christ, and through Him to all mankind.[2]

What Loves Requires

God not only identifies with the poor and downtrodden, he commands that we live in a loving relationship with each other.

"He who has two coats, let him share with him who has none; and he who has food, let him do likewise" (Luke 3:11). "Owe no one anything, except to love one another; for he who loves his neighbor has fulfilled the law" (Rom. 13:8). The law under Christ is just one: love.

> Beloved, let us love one another; for love is of God, and he who loves is born of God and knows God. He who does not love does not know God; for God is love. . . . If any one says, "I love God," and hates his brother . . . whom he has seen, cannot love God whom he has not seen. And this commandment we have from him, that he who loves

God should love his brother also (1 John 4:7-8,20-21).

The amazing Christian ethic of love with its uncompromising demand requires us to examine our whole set of values.

In the first two chapters we looked at the tremendous abundance that most of us enjoy. We have seen in chapter 3 that we are stewards of all that God has given us, even the other nine tenths. We have seen that God identifies with the poor and commands us to love others and to give to meet their needs. Let us now consider the vast needs that face our communities and our world.

The Need

Did you know that

1. Approximately thirty-five million Americans live under the poverty level of $774 per month for a nonrural family of four?

2. There are also 35-40 million near-poor who need help with shelter, food, jobs, income, and medical care?

3. In early 1983 twelve million Americans were unemployed?

4. Frustrated people are begging for work in New York?

5. The poverty level is 70 percent in Chicago, where more than a thousand people lined up at Chicago's Uptown Baptist Church to receive food baskets?

6. In Cleveland 110,000 people receive emergency food relief and another 45,000 need food assistance?

7. One out of every five children in the United States lives in poverty?

8. Nearly seven million children have no known health care and one child in three has never seen a dentist?

9. Nearly one billion people, almost one out of every four persons on the earth, live in a state of absolute poverty?

10. Almost twenty million people die each year of starvation or hunger-related illnesses?

11. Of that twenty million about twelve million of them are children who die before they reach the age of five?

12. *Each day* about thirty thousand children starve to death?

13. Twenty-eight human beings die of starvation each minute?

14. More people starve to death in three days than were killed at Hiroshima?

15. Eight hundred million people are on the threshold of starvation?

16. Starvation has killed more people in the last five years than all the wars, murders, and revolutions of the last century?

17. A billion people exist on this earth on per capita incomes of less than $150 per year?

18. In spite of the population explosion, enough food is currently being produced to meet the basic calorie requirements of every person on earth?

19. Three- and four-year-old children must work to help support their starving families in Bangladesh?

Ninety percent of their 100 million people earn less than $88 per year.

20. Every month 12,000 Afghan refugees pour into 250 refugee camps in Northern Pakistan in search of freedom?

21. Upper Volta has experienced a great drought; trees and animals are dying; water reserves are very low?

22. In Honduras and other countries children's bellies are bloated by worms picked up in dirty water?

23. Bushfires are igniting dry fields in Ghana, which is struggling to resettle a million of its people recently expelled from Nigeria?

24. In Southern India, where rice is the staff of life, drought is wreaking havoc? Heavy rains have destroyed much of the wheat crop to the north?

25. Latin America suffers floods, earthquakes, and more drought?

> In 1977 the National Academy of Sciences published a study stating that "seven hundred and fifty million people in the poorest nations live in extreme poverty with annual incomes of less than $75." In the U.S., on the other hand, middle-class people often feel poor when they make only $15,000, $18,000, or even $25,000 each year. We are fourteen times as rich as the average person in India, and the gap continues to widen.[3]

While the average income in the United States is well above the amount necessary for an adequate lifestyle, many Americans don't have enough income to provide the basic necessities of life, such as adequate nutrition, clothing, housing, and medical care.

No one knows how many people in America are truly hungry. The last governmental nutrition survey was completed in 1978. The next one will be taken this year (1985). It is easier to tell who is poor than who is hungry, but soup kitchen lines have been growing.[4]

The Proof Is Action

Three times Jesus asked Peter (John 21:15-17), "Do you love me?" Peter always replied the same way, "Lord, you know that I love you." And each time, Jesus gave him the same challenge, "Feed my sheep." Obviously, Jesus was not asking Peter simply to provide literal food for his people. I believe he was saying *care* for my people, which involves being concerned for their spiritual, emotional, and physical needs. A good test of our love for Christ is always the same: it's how we respond to others in His name that counts.

The proof of what we say is in the doing. If we claim to love the Lord, if we claim to love His people, why are we so willing to have so much for ourselves and be satisfied with so little for our neighbors? Do we spend our money on things we don't need and allow others to go without the real necessities of life? Is our philosophy of giving "a microwave oven for me, a can of beans for you"?

I find it difficult to teach the occasional Sunday School lesson on meeting human need if I haven't personally made an attempt to help the needy women in my class. I could tell them week after week what the Bible says about Christians caring, but if all I do in addition to my tithe is bring a few canned goods for a Thanksgiving basket, my efforts are in vain. I might as well not teach at all; I might be doing more damage than good for the cause of Christ. I can take my seat with the Pharisees.

We can fool ourselves about who or what we love, but we can't fool the Lord. I doubt that we can fool the needy world either. In our modesty, we don't wear sheer nylon clothing because we know people could see right through it. Why then are we so naive when it comes to our giving? Isn't it obvious that people in need see right through our sham when we say, "We love you in Christ," yet we continue to have so much while they have so little?

> If a brother or sister is ill-clad and in lack of daily food, and one of you says to them, "Go in peace, be warmed and filled," without giving them the things needed for the body, what does it profit? So faith by itself, if it has no works, is dead" (Jas. 2:15-17).

Talk is cheap! Sometimes we can be so "heavenly minded" that we're no "earthly good."

> But if anyone has the world's goods and sees his brother in need, yet closes his heart against him, how does God's love abide in him? Little children,

> let us not love in word or speech but in deed and in truth (1 John 3:17-18).

Don Francisco, contemporary gospel singer, makes the same statement in a different way: "Love is not a feeling—it's an act of your will."[5] Love is more than an *emotion*, it is something *we do. What we do* gives testimony to *whose we are.* Christians belong to the Lord.

If we really love the Lord the way that we claim to, we would care about the things He cares about; our Lord was and is concerned about people because He loves us. He loves *all* of us. He hurts when His people hurt. Our relationship with the Lord will depend when, as we see others hurting, we hurt, too. But that's just the beginning: we must care enough to respond, to reach out, to help. We are Christ's instruments; we are called out for this very purpose.

Tony Campolo, preacher, sociologist, college instructor, and disciple of our Lord, tells a story I'd like to share with you. He and some other dedicated Christians have started an orphanage in Haiti to provide food and medical treatment for some of the many children who are literally starving to death in that country. Because of a lack of supplies, facilities, and staff, they can only handle fifty children at a time. As they went to one village in Haiti to receive the fifty children they were greeted by five hundred children with bloated stomachs and bones for arms and legs. The children wanted so much to show their appreciation for what these Christians were trying to do for them that they had learned a song to sing for their potential rescuers. They sang the chorus, "God Is So Good."

In that very touching moment, Tony and his team were asked to pick fifty children from the five hundred that stood before him. He knew that in choosing fifty, he was dooming four hundred and fifty to almost certain death. How could he make a choice like that? He was so torn by the overwhelming experience that as soon as he had some quiet time alone he began to pray. "Father in heaven, how could you allow this to happen? Why aren't you doing something about these starving children?" And after a few anguished moments, God's answer came: "I'm doing the best I can. You see, I just don't have enough people."

This forces us to ask ourselves some questions: Does God have us? Can He use us to work His purposes in the world? Will we choose to play it safe and say, "Get someone else, Lord?" Are we short on love when it comes to people we don't know?

Robert E. Bingham remarks in *A Cup of Cold Water,*

> What a shame that the Christian church has sometimes forsaken its responsibility to minister to the disadvantaged! The united funds, community chests, and multiple other drives have filled the vacuum—but not always in Jesus' name. Even if such gifts are given in the spirit of Christ, they are not always so recognized by the ultimate recipient.[6]

Hunger and need are real in our world. It's time that Christians did something about it. It's hard for people to hear the gospel, much less believe it, if they haven't had enough to eat for days on end. Beth Hayworth wrote:

> Hunger is real in America. It may be hidden in the rural dirt roads or in the urban back-street shacks, but it is real and it is a spiritual albatross around our nation's neck. For those among us who are called to do God's work here on earth, the task is clear. We have seen the need—now is the time to act.[7]

Now *is* the time for us to act: to live out the love of Christ in our world.

---

1. Sider, p. 164.
2. Werning, pp. 67-68.
3. Sider, p. 14.
4. Beth Spring, "Is There Hunger in America?" *Christianity Today* (March 16, 1984), pp. 28-32.
5. Don Francisco, "Love Is not a Feeling," *Don Francisco: The Live Concert* (Nashville: New Pax Records, 1982).
6. Robert E. Bingham, *A Cup of Cold Water* (Nashville: Convention Press, 1971), p. 7.
7. Beth Hayworth, *The Baptist Student* (Nashville: Convention Press, April, 1970), p. 14.

Not Conformed to This World

Do not be conformed to this world but be transformed by the renewal of your mind, that you may prove what is the will of God, what is good and acceptable and perfect (Rom. 12:2).

"If it hasn't already done so, the church in the 1980's must recognize that it lives in a pagan society; it must seek for values and norms not shared by society. In short, it will either recover the Christian doctrine of nonconformity or cease to have any authentic Christian voice."[1]

Paul urges Christians to be different than the world we live in. No, we are not to try to cut ourselves off from the world, we must live in it. I don't believe that God meant us to be hermits living in a cave or monks locked up in a monastery. Our relationship with others in this world is a very important part of what it means to be a Christian.

However, we are not to conform to this world. Its goals, its pleasures, its attitudes, its morals, its values, and its loves must not be ours.

> Do not love the world or the things in the world. If any one loves the world, love for the Father is not in him. For all that is in the world, the lust of

> the flesh and the lust of the eyes and the pride of life, is not of the Father but is of the world. And the world passes away, and the lust of it; but he who does the will of God abides for ever (1 John 2:15-17).

In *The Practical Message of James,* Howard Colson states,

> Every human being has two rivals for the love and allegiance of his heart—God and the world. To put selfish indulgence first in our lives is to be the world's lover, not God's. . . .
>
> One of the gravest problems facing churches today grows out of the fact that multitudes of their members are dabbling in worldliness; some are even wallowing in it. If we could persuade professing Christians to shun worldliness and live as Jesus wants us to live, we would eliminate one of the greatest barriers to the Christian movement.[2]

Since most of us in the United States were Americans before we were Christians, we have brought to the Christian life a great deal of baggage that might have been better left behind. When we agreed to let Jesus be our pilot for life, I'm sure there was a big sign in the airport saying, "No carry-on luggage, please." We probably ignored the sign and brought with us a culture that was most unlike that of the first-century Christians.

A person doesn't need to live in the first century to

be a Christian. Christianity is not limited by time frame or culture. Neither do we need to completely deny the culture of which we are a part. For example, Chinese Christians need not become Americanized or Judaized to feel they are authentic Christians.

But when we give our lives to Christ, something happens to us. Jesus makes us new creatures in Him. We are changed: our attitudes, our values, and our goals are different. But we must be careful, Satan has just begun to fight! He urges us to hang on to our old attitudes, our old values, and our old goals. Although the victory has been won, the contest is not over.

We live daily with the challenge to be different, not for the sake of being different, but in the life-style of Jesus, who said, "If any man would come after me, let him deny himself and take up his cross and follow me. For whoever would save his life will lose it; and whoever loses his life for my sake and the gospel's will save it" (Mark 8:34*b*-35).

The Amish people are a community of people who for religious reasons have refused to conform with this society. Is there anything that we can learn from them?

Learning from the Amish

Living in South Central Pennsylvania as I do, it is not unusual to see Amish people as well as other Plain People going about their daily tasks from time to time. In our highly industrialized, mechanized, and scientific society, the Amish are a group of people who place a premium on a fixed social structure, stability, and simplicity rather than our change or advancement. They seem content without so many of the world stresses and allurements that we take for granted. They focus on their needs which are their everyday requirements. They are self-sufficient in their community, and they rarely reach beyond it.

In 250 years Amish customs, methods of transportation, farming, and entertainment have changed insignificantly. They practice a life of self-denial and separation from the world. They are stewards of the land and work the soil. "Next to the Bible and his religion, the land is the most important thing in an Amishman's life. It is the physical manifestation of a gift from God given over to man's safekeeping."[3] These are the words of John M. Zielinski from his recent book, *The Amish Across America.*

Unlike non-Amish farmers who employ power equipment to get the job done, the Amish make use of animal and human power to work the fields. Waterwheels and massive, old steam engines are two exceptions to the rule. Horsepower seems to be their main source of power apart from themselves.

"Old age pensions, social security, and insurance are not sanctioned because their people rally around one in need, or in an emergency. They have a profound respect for one another and their God, which is the catalyst for their existence in our contemporary world."[4]

By using this brief portrait of the Amish life-style, I am not advocating that we as Christians in North

America follow suit. We are not called to live separately from the world in a geographical sense. We cannot all depend on farming for our livelihoods. If we use them wisely, I see no real value in rejecting energy sources such as electricity and fuels or in dressing so similarly as long as we are not tempted to put too great a value on clothing.

Rather, I mention the life-style of the Amish as food for thought. In attempting to be different from the world, the Amish cling to some biblical values that we "modernized" Christians could learn from.

First, the Amish have a strong sense of stewardship. This stewardship is a grateful response to what God has given them.

Second, they live a simple, unmaterialistic life-style, in which the pursuit of things does not choke out the really important values in life. Although these people work hard physically, I imagine there is more time left for relationships, communication, and good times than in an average contemporary family, which has all the "things" it needs to make life easier.

Finally, they live in community, sharing with and helping each other. This, by the way, is clearly a description of the early church. We are called, not to be exclusive, but to care.

Why Be Different?

Why should we be different in the first place? For one reason, God's Word says that we should be different.

We have already read the injunctions in Romans 12:2 and 1 John 2:15-17.

We should *live* differently because we *are* different. We have been with Jesus. That should make all the difference. "Now when they saw the boldness of Peter and John, and perceived that they were uneducated, common men, they wondered; and they recognized that they had been with Jesus" (Acts 4:13). If only people could see Jesus making a difference in us!

We should live differently because Jesus is our Lord. A contemporary television show portrays the master of a Far Eastern religion teaching his follower (disciple). The young disciple not only follows his master as he travels, but he takes on his life-style and purposes. Being a disciple is a full-time pursuit, which touches us in every area of our lives.

This kind of lordship is what the rich young ruler was not able to accept (Matt. 19:16-22; Luke 18:18-23). Let's look at his situation for some insights for ourselves concerning material things and conformity.

The rich young man approached Jesus with sincerity and respect and asked Him what he must do to get eternal life. It appears that this man was truly seeking; he knew something was missing in his life. Jesus told him to keep the Commandments. The young man asked which Commandments he should keep. Jesus cited the Commandments which deal with human relationships; He did not include those that deal with man's relationship to God. The young man claimed that he had kept all of those from his childhood. He obviously considered himself a godly man. We really don't know what kind of relationship he had with others. We can only guess.

Finally, Jesus told the rich young man that in order to have eternal life he must sell all that he possessed and give it to the poor, and then, come and follow Him. At first glance, it would appear that this indicates a kind of salvation by works, while Paul clearly holds that our salvation is by faith, not works. Jesus is not saying that we can earn our salvation in this passage. He is saying that in receiving salvation, we are not inviting him in as Savior *only,* but as Lord. And if we are to do this, He must come first in our lives. While He does not ask everyone to sell one's possessions, He did ask it of the rich young ruler because Jesus, in His wisdom, could see that he placed great value on his wealth. We could say he almost worshiped his possessions. The Lord realized that if the things the young man owned had first place in his life, Jesus would have to take second place. So Jesus asked the young man to give up what he prized most to follow Him.

Waldo Werning says,

> Covetousness permeates our natural state. We are born to care for ourselves, and we do not easily shed the inborn characteristics that drive us on in a relentless search for self-satisfaction. The stewardship message of the Gospel collides head-on with our natural instincts about what is "good" for ourselves.[5]

This passage about the rich young man, which contains many important truths, says something significant about materialism and also about conformity. The truth that stands out for our purposes is that Jesus requires first place in our hearts and lives. This truth, although inescapable, brought me to an insight which I had not really seen before. In our holier-than-thou attitude, we are likely to see this story unfold and pity the poor man who could not make the wiser choice. I wonder if we had the same choice, would we be able to put aside our accumulation of money and things and choose Christ? Are we just as enamored by our possessions as was the rich young man even though we may not be as wealthy as he? Are we trying to straddle the fence and have both? Fortunately, when we come to Christ he doesn't demand that *we* make that choice—or does he? We can have all of our selfish desires and still belong to Christ as long as we give a tenth. Or can we? Could we be guilty of wanting to "have our cake and eat it, too"?

Jesus was asking this man to do something very unconventional. Everyone knows that if you have great wealth you don't give it all away and go follow someone who has no place to lay His head. If you have a lot of money, you show it off with fine clothes and possessions. If you have riches, you invest it and make more riches. You certainly don't give it all away!

Jesus was asking the man to be different, to take on a new life-style that would show the world that he belonged to Jesus. But he couldn't do it.

Jesus didn't ask the young man in the passage to give just because there were needy people in his town (you can be sure there were), but because giving generously was important to his own spiritual growth. He needed to be freed from the tangle of material things, to step out in faith in his commitment to Christ, to demonstrate that Christ would be first in his life. But he couldn't do it. Could we?

> We tend to agree with Clement of Alexandria that the important part is *attitude* toward wealth per se. Can there be a true inward attitude without outward consequences? Is it not hypocrisy to teach one way and live another?[6]

Although the ruler was sincere in his question, he could not trust Jesus until he ceased trusting in riches.

> In this day when vast multitudes of people are wealthy by comparison, every Christian needs to examine his life to determine how much he depends or trusts in riches. It is not just the extremely wealthy who come to trust in their wealth, but the man of modest means who cannot part with a portion of his wealth may also fail the test of discipleship because of his trust in material things.[7]

Do we all to some degree trust in material things?

E. Fred Savage, Jr., says, "Exercise greater faith in God. Believe that he will supply our needs. This will keep us from selfishly laying up or amassing great treasures on earth."[8] Let us act on faith that God will supply our needs so that we can generously give to share the gospel with a lost world.

The rich young man was a man living utterly selfishly. His real god was comfort. He lacked a spirit of self-denial. Have we also left self-denial out of our following Jesus in the twentieth century?

Sacrifice

Sacrifice is a dirty word. Like "giving," we try not to talk about it. We would like to leave it out of our relationship to Christ. It is doubtful that many of us will be asked to give up our lives for the cause of Christ, yet sacrifice is inherent in following one who said, "If any man would come after me, let him deny himself and take up his cross and follow me" (Mark 8:34*b*).

Unlike the rich young ruler, Zacchaeus (Luke 19:1-10) was one who was willing to take the risk that was involved in following Christ. He is a positive illustration of one whose new relationship with Christ altered his response to material things. It appeared that he had gained some of his wealth unjustly, and he was seeking to make it right, following his encounter with Christ. Besides that, Jesus gave him a new willingness to give that replaced his desire to get.

We Christians speak about what a difference Jesus can make in a person's life. Do we really believe it? Should we be surprised to see many more modern Zacchaeus's? When we give our lives to Christ, are we satisfied to give him just the "spiritual part" (as if there were such a part) and continue business as usual with the "material part"?

Sacrificial giving is the keynote of one of the most familiar stories in the New Testament, the widow's mite. It is a story we use to teach our children that their gifts, however small, are of great value in God's eyes. It is not the amount, but the thought that counts. The woman gave two small coins, the smallest coins in human history, which valued about eight cents total in American coinage. Yet Jesus said her's was the best gift, better than the gifts of the rich who gave large sums. What was the difference? The difference was that she gave generously out of the little that she had while others gave little in proportion to their abundance. She gave all she had.

"Why the Chimes Rang" is a short story, often used at Christmas, in which a young boy sacrifices a long-awaited opportunity in order to help an old woman freezing in the snow. It is a poignant story that makes us face the reality of our own self-centeredness. There is one statement in the story, that, I think, more than any other, speaks to God's people in our time: "Every Christmas Eve the rich people still crowded to the altar, each one trying to bring some better gift than any other, without giving anything that he wanted for himself."[9]

We can never come close to matching the sacrifice that Jesus made for us. However, I believe, unselfish giving for the cause of Christ is part of what Paul meant when he said, "Do not be conformed to this world" (Rom. 12:2*a*). "Don't spend your money the way the world does" is my very free translation of this verse as it applies to this subject.

Are we Christians really any different than the world? I wonder if we have sold ourselves a bill of goods by telling ourselves that we can be Christians and have it all, too. Are we fence-straddlers, trying to enjoy the benefits of both life-styles?

Several years ago when bumper stickers were particularly popular, I was often stirred to see the one reading, "Honk, if you love Jesus." It always gave me a thrill to know that the owner of the other car was also a Christian, even though I didn't know the person. Later, in reaction to that bumper sticker, I began to see another bumper sticker, which read, "If you love Jesus, tithe. Anybody can honk." I was struck by those simple words: if you love Jesus, do something that really counts! Be willing to pay the price (see Luke 14:26-33).

The way of the kingdom does not conform to the way of the world. What this means in terms of stewardship is beautifully expressed in the lyrics of a song by Gary Davis:

The Kingdom Way

God doesn't bless us that we might build our kingdoms
God doesn't bless us to promote good good feelings
He doesn't bless us to keep it all for ourselves.

In this age of greed and selfishness
Most people strive for all they can possess.
They build their treasures with things that fade away.

Our Lord has shown us the way of the Kingdom.
He did not have a place to lay His head.
He said the happy ones are those who learn
to give as they have freely received.

Chorus
That's why our God blesses us. That we might be a
blessing.
God our God gives to us that we might
give to those in need.
That all the ends of the earth will know.
That all the ends of the earth will know.
That he is God, That he is God, That He, That He is God.

Only two things in all creation
will remain throughout eternity,
The Word of God and the souls of men.

As God does prosper you with things He has made
Don't try to cling to them. Don't you become their slave.
Set your affections on things which are above.

He owns the world and all it contains.
He is the One Who gives and takes away.
He gives us good gifts and we gladly receive.
As we look around we give to those in need.[10]

---

1. Willard Swartley, "Mennonite Higher Education Facing the 1980's" *Gospel Herald* (September 26, 1978), p. 726.
2. Howard Colson, *The Practical Message of James* (Nashville: Broadman Press, 1969), pp. 67-68.
3. John M. Zielinski, *The Amish Across America* (Grinnell, Iowa: Amish Heritage Publishing Co., 1983), p. 72.
4. Donald Denlinger and James A. Warner, *The Gentle People: A Portrait of the Amish* (New York: Grossman Publishers, 1969), p. 13.
5. Werning, pp. 73-74.
6. Sider, p. 43.
7. N. F. Greer, *Stewardship Scripture Studies,* Vol. 3 (Nashville: n.p., 1971), pp. 66-67.

8. E. Fred Savage, Jr., *Stewardship Scripture Studies* Vol. 2 (Nashville: n.p., 1971), p. 29.

9. Raymond M. Alden, *Why the Chimes Rang* (New York: Bobbs-Merrill Co. Inc., 1954), p. 6.

10. Gary Davis, "The Kingdom Way," *Numbered Days* (Costa Mesa, Calif.: Ministry Resource Center, 1983).

A Bathtub and a Cookpot

He who has more than he needs is a thief.
—Gandhi

When the Lord provided manna to feed His people in the wilderness (Ex. 16:16-20), He told each family to gather as much as they needed for the day. He reminded them not to gather more than they needed with the idea of saving it for the next day. Everyone had just enough, but those who disobeyed God and tried to store up and hoard the manna for "a rainy day" found their manna full of worms and rotten. There is a lesson here about obedience to God as well as materialism for Christians. If we obey Him, God will provide our needs. We must trust in Him for guidance, not ourselves. We must consider what we need, not just what we want. I wonder if our preoccupation with possessions beyond our needs is rotten in God's eyes?

If you tried to reduce what you now own to what you really need, what would you have left? How many of the possessions that you now have do you really need? I'm certain you would have more on your list than "just a bathtub and a cookpot." I expect our lists would be different and varied in length. Much depends on what we value most, and, also, our own standard of living.

What is standard of living? A dictionary definition might say it is a grade or level of subsistence and comfort in everyday life enjoyed by a community, class, or individual. A minimum standard is that which sustains human life, and even this varies because of climate and geography. What is accepted as a poor standard for a group of people in one country might be considered good in another. Interestingly enough, there doesn't seem to be a maximum limit. The capacity to increase one's standard of living to coincide with one's income is almost limitless. We must ask ourselves, Are our salaries the only limits to our life-style?

What are we teaching our children about life-style? Are we passing on our wasteful attitudes to the next generation who may live in a world of scarcity as adults? From generation to generation, parents have always wanted their children to have it better than they did, and in the twenties and thirties that was probably legitimate. But now there are more comforts than we need. The wise parents will teach their children unselfish and unmaterialistic values by example and explanation.

Charles Chaney says,

> We live in a secular society. Secular values and goals have invaded our churches and fashioned the value system of individual Christians. The average American Christian may be more of a slave

> to the material than the most doctrinaire Communist in Russia. Our Churches stand in need of a *theology of material possessions.*[1]

What does the Bible say about material things? Does the Bible teach a specific standard of living for Christians? What measure of life's possessions should a person have? Should the Christian standard differ from others, and, if so, to what extent and in what ways? Does the Bible recognize a place for luxuries in life? Should a Christian be expected to give up conveniences of living for his faith?

The Bible does not set out specific principles concerning how we should spend our money, however, there are some guidelines dealing with possessions and money.

The Bible does not say that material possessions are good or evil, neither does it condemn possessions, nor the possessing of material things. It recognizes something more than bread in a person's life. The Scriptures accept the idea of personal ownership and inheritance, but they also call for a way of life in which the Christians cannot enjoy the advantages without being concerned about the disadvantages and sufferings of others. The Bible also recognizes no purpose for abundance other than as a means of service. "Let the thief no longer steal, but rather let him labor, doing honest work with his hands, so that he may be able to give to those in need" (Eph. 4:28). This does not mean we are to give away all we earn, but that with our abundance comes the obligation to service. We should use the abilities God has given us to make money and spend it wisely for two purposes: to meet the needs of humanity and to bring people to God through Jesus Christ. By committing our lives to fulfilling God's purposes for material possessions here on earth, we will be laying "up for [ourselves] treasures in heaven" (Matt. 6:20*a*).

The Bible, however, labels luxury and wealth as extremely hazardous because of what they tend to do to the person who has them. Matthew 6:24 and 19:22 indicate that money and possessions can restrict our freedom. If we become servants of money and materialism, we cannot serve God at the same time. John V. Taylor, in his book, *Enough Is Enough,* has something to say about possessions and freedom:

> Our enemy is not possessions but excess. Our battle-cry is not "Nothing!" but "Enough!" But the defiant simplicity we need is essentially of the same spirit as the poverty which St. Francis sought with such ardour. It consists of the ability to do without for the sake of freedom.[2]

Wealth and luxury can also blind us to the needs of others. The story of the rich man and Lazarus (Luke 16:19-21) is a good biblical example of this truth. On this subject Don Helder Camara has said:

> I used to think when I was a child, that Christ might have been exaggerating when he warned

about the dangers of wealth. Today I know better. I know how very hard it is to be rich and still keep the milk of human kindness. Money has a dangerous way of putting scales on one's eyes, a dangerous way of freezing people's hands, eyes, lips, and hearts."[3]

Ronald J. Sider comments,

> The Old Testament does not tell us specifically whether we should buy a better car, keep the one we have or have no car at all. It does not tell us whether we should upgrade our lifestyle by getting a bigger house, or cut it back by getting a smaller one. It doesn't specify exactly what our lifestyle should be. Rather, it gives us certain principles by which we must measure our lifestyle. To face those principles honestly and prayerfully is bound to lead to changes that will help us simplify our lives in order to be more obedient disciples of our Lord.[4]

Here are some biblical principles to consider.

1. All things belong to God (Ex. 19:5).
2. Those who belong to God should not be concerned primarily about material things (Matt. 6:25-34; Luke 12:15).
3. The hoarding of wealth is contrary to God's call to self-giving (2 Cor. 8:9).
4. Christians must be willing to forsake all they have to follow Christ (Mark 8:34-36; Matt. 19:21).

5. The Christian must use moral judgment in determining what is enough for personal needs (Eccl. 5;13, 16-17).

6. Material response to the poor and hungry is a test of Christian experience, genuine love, and authentic righteousness (Jas. 2:15-17).

7. Those who neglect people in need will come under God's judgment (Matt. 25:41-46; Luke 16:19-25).

8. Christians are to treat others as they want to be treated themselves (Matt. 7:12).

9. Christians should not waste money on transient pleasures (Luke 15:13-14).

10. Jesus regards giving as a wise investment (Matt. 6:19-21).

I can hear people asking, "Are you saying that we should become poor just because other people are poor?" It is a personal decision each Christian must make. Our family is still struggling with it. We have a good example in our Lord himself. "For you know the grace of our Lord Jesus Christ, that though he was rich, yet for your sake he became poor, so that by his poverty you might become rich" (2 Cor. 8:9).

Ronald Sider points up this hard to swallow truth: "As Christians we have given up our rights to choose, to indulge our preferences or to follow our fancies. We have committed ourselves to lives pleasing to the One who has bought us and owns us and has the right to order our consumption patterns."[5]

In *Living More with Less,* Doris Longacre writes, "The most under-utilized resource to aid in simple living is our own heads."[6] She says small ideas and acts give us a place to start.

Let's get practical. What are some of the ways that we can be good stewards of all that God has given us? What measures can we take to live more simply?

1. Conserve energy in your home and in your car.

2. Don't carry much money with you from day to day. It's too easily spent on things you don't need just because you have it with you.

3. Don't be a shopper. Avoid stores and shopping centers unless you really need something. Make a list and stick to it when you shop. Don't be tricked into impulse buying. Merchants know us: that is why they put many small items around the check out counters so we'll be tempted to buy more while we're waiting in line.

4. Make use of solar energy where you can. That doesn't always mean a big investment of money. It could mean hanging your laundry out to dry instead of using a dryer year-round.

5. Try to repair things instead of always throwing them away and buying new.

6. Plant a garden. Freeze and can your own food as you are able.

7. Recycle bags and other paper goods.

8. Find out where the closest recycling station is to you and use it.

9. Eat less red meat and more nutritional foods. Eating more chicken and fish and less beef is good stewardship of food sources. Poultry and seafood are less

fattening, anyway. Some people have chosen vegetarianism for reasons of health and stewardship as well.

10. Don't overeat; eat wisely.

11. About 80 percent of today's diseases are linked to frantic living. Slow down your living.

12. Walk or ride a bike as often as you can.

13. Get serious about your own part in pollution and littering.

14. Be frugal. Find uses for leftovers.

15. When you buy, buy things that last so they won't need to be replaced so often.

16. If possible, choose part-time work to allow time for serving others.

17. Use less disposables.

18. Use few kitchen appliances.

19. Value family and friendship above money.

20. Be willing to learn from the poor about life-style and stewardship of God's gifts. After all, we follow someone who was born in a stable and died between thieves.

21. Avoid the use of credit cards. If necessary, to escape the temptation, get rid of them. Credit cards encourage impulsive buying and, often, bring trouble later on.

22. Analyze your *real* clothes needs.

23. Don't go out and buy something because you are lonely, bored, or feel the need to be rewarded. Do something for someone else instead. You'll be rewarded in a more lasting way.

24. When you sense that you "need" something new,

try to think of an alternative so that you don't actually have to buy something new, but will have your purpose served anyway.

25. Insulate your home. It will cost you some money, but it's worth it in the long haul.

26. Learn to cook with a pressure cooker. It saves time and energy. Use a lid when cooking, for the same reasons.

27. Keep account of what and how you spend your money for a two-week period. Then evaluate your use of it.

28. Help start a children's clothing exchange in your church or neighborhood.

29. Learn to cut your family members' hair at home. It will save you money, gas, and time.

30. Initiate or be involved with a food cooperative.

31. Make a stand for less expensive, simpler facilities for churches.

32. Discuss economic discipleship in your church regularly.

33. Find ways to conserve water, especially hot water.

34. Turn off lights when not in use.

35. Make use of garbage in a compost pile for your garden.

36. Don't get carried away with "clean." It's a time guzzler.

37. Recycle glass, paper, and aluminum.

38. Buy biodegradable products and materials as much as possible.

39. Make some of your own cleaning supplies. For example, one part household ammonia and three parts parts water makes a fine window cleaner at much less expense than the commercial brands.

40. Try simple camping.

41. Drive your car less.

42. Buy a gas-efficient car the next time you need a car.

43. Give favors, trips, and so forth, for gifts rather than "things."

44. Make up games and entertainment that don't require monetary expenditures.

45. Familiarize yourself with the facts of overconsumption and individualization in our culture.

46. Talk about your resources and your responsibility with your family members. Help them understand what you are trying to do and why you are doing it.

47. Talk with others frequently who are attempting to simplify their life-styles. Read books and magazines on the issue.

48. Make simplicity a challenge. Allow it to be fun.

49. As you earn more money, don't be tempted to raise your living standard along with it.

50. If you spend much time browsing through catalogs or advertisements which come in the mail, you'll be sure to find items that you "need." Avoid them.

51. Support government food policies committed to world food security and rural development for small farmers in food-deficit countries.

The quality of our lives will seem higher than ever

before when we turn away from this materialistic culture and simplify our lives. Start now or you may never do it.

Thrift has some negative connotations in our society. To be thrifty need not necessarily mean to be stingy. Phyllis McGinley, in her book, *Sixpence in Her Shoe,* speaks to that point:

> Thrift is neither selfishness nor cheeseparing, but a large compassionate attribute, a just reward for God's material gifts. It has nothing in common with meanness and is different from economy, which, although it may assist thrift, is a habit rather than a moral. . . . Economy saves pennies, trims corners, and has a tidy mind. . . . The poor receive economy's handouts, but they will be relentlessly entered on a tax return. Meanness ruthlessly stints the table, lets others pay the check, and when it gives old coats to refugee committees, cuts off buttons and fur collars. Thrift is something else again. When thrift serves stew to the family to ease the budget, it sees to it that the dish is savory as filet mignon and it delights to share with anyone who comes to the door. It is never stingy and antlike. Thrift is a preserver rather than a hoarder and rejoices in hospitality.[7]

At the Lausanne Congress for World Evangelism, the U.S. Consultation on Simple Lifestyle got its start. The congress, possibly the largest international gathering of Evangelical Christians ever assembled, pledged themselves to renewed efforts in the task of world evangelism. One of the goals they set for themselves was that of encouraging affluent Christians to choose simpler life-styles. The Lausanne Covenant, in part, grew out of that goal. Paragraph nine of the Covenant reads: "All of us are shocked by the poverty of millions and disturbed by the injustices which cause it. Those of us who live in affluent circumstances accept our duty to develop a simple lifestyle in order to contribute generously to both relief and evangelism."[8]

Ronald Sider further clarifies the goal:

> The Lausanne Covenant states the proper motivation for simpler living. Christians are not committed to a simple lifestyle. We are committed to Jesus Christ and his kingdom and thus to faithful participation in the mission of our servant King in a lost, broken world. It is because more than two and a half billion people have never heard the gospel and because up to one billion are starving or malnourished that Western Christians today must drastically simplify our lifestyles.[9]

Although we live in a consumption-oriented, success-driven society, we must return to and seek after New Testament values. We must examine our wants to see if they are really luxuries and examine our needs to see if they aren't just wants in disguise. An accurate inventory should free resources to share with others. A true biblical life-style is one of caring, sharing, and self-giving.

There is hope for us yet. An interest in returning to voluntary simplicity has already begun in North America. A Harris poll in 1977 indicated that 79 percent of North Americans were concerned about living with basic essentials and only 17 percent would support "reaching higher standards of living."

The term *recycle* is part of the language of those who espouse simple living. It should not be foreign to those of us who are the body of Christ. We also have been "recycled." We are new creatures in Him. Our own need to be recycled is the subject of this poem by Joyce M. Shutt.

Consumers' Prayer

throwaway bottles
throwaway cans
throwaway friendships
throwaway fans

disposable diapers
disposable plates
disposable people
disposable wastes

instant puddings
instant rice
instant intimacy
instant ice

plastic dishes
plastic laces
plastic flowers
plastic faces

Lord of the Living
transcending our lives
infuse us with meaning
recycle our lives[10]

---

1. Charles Chaney, *Stewardship Scripture Studies,* Vol. 2 (Nashville: n.p., 1971), p. 10.
2. John V. Taylor, *Enough Is Enough* (Minneapolis, Minn.: Augsburg Publishing House, 1977), p. 82.
3. *Revolution through Peace* (New York: Harper & Row, 1971), p. 142.
4. Ronald J. Sider, pp. 38-39.
5. Ronald J. Sider, p. 99.
6. Longacre, p. 49.
7. Phyllis McGinley, *Sixpence in Her Shoe* (New York: Dell Publishing Co., 1965), pp. 80-81.
8. Ronald J. Sider, p. 13.
9. Ronald J. Sider, p. 13.
10. Longacre, p. 14. Used by permission Herald Press.

What Do We Need?

Caring precedes sharing.

We are no longer under the law, but under Christ. There are no absolute laws other than the law of love that can tell us to whom or how much to give. What do we need in our lives to make those kinds of judgments in accord with God's plan?

First, we need eyes that see. I don't mean that we need 20/20 vision, but we need eyes that do more than just photograph the external world in our brains. We need eyes that process what they see and, once processed, respond. Eyes that see involve more than a biological process.

Our children often tell us that they didn't hear us when we question them about some instruction that was given earlier. The reality is that they heard us, but they didn't listen. A similar phenomenon occurs when we see. Our biological eyes are seeing all the time our eyes are open, but they are not always taking in what they see.

God is critical of those who have eyes, but don't see. "Hear this, O foolish and senseless people,/who have eyes, but see not, who have ears but hear not" (Jer. 5:21). "Blessed are the eyes which see what you see! For I tell you that many prophets and kings desired to see what you see, and did not see it, and to hear what you hear, and did not hear it" (Luke 10:23*b*-24).

Although many of us share the same abundant blessings and the same needy world, I am constantly amazed that while some see it, others do not.

Second, we need a heart with compassion. God's Word clearly calls us to compassion (Matt. 25:35-40; 1 John 3:17-18; Luke 3:11; Jas. 2:15-17). "And whoever gives to one of these little ones even a cup of cold water because he is a disciple, truly, I say to you, he shall not lose his reward" (Matt. 10:42).

In *The Practical Message of James,* Howard Colson says that one of the three tests of religion is compassion toward the unfortunate. He says that "the three tests of real religion do not concern doctrine at all but are the practical expression of the inner life of one who is in vital touch with Jesus Christ."[1]

He goes on to say that a major issue has always been the inadequacy of a dead faith. Love in action was James' main concern here, and it is always at the heart of Jesus' teaching.

Jesus' parable of the good Samaritan not only answered the question, "Who is my neighbor?" but contrasted the compassion of a particular Samaritan with the lack of compassion of a particular priest and a Levite, who also passed that way. It is interesting to note that both the priest and the Levite represented the religious groups of the day. They probably considered themselves among the righteous of their time. What does this parable say to Christians today? Are we sometimes more pious than compassionate?

A store carrying pornographic books and films recently opened adjacent to an attractive residential neighborhood. A local group, composed of many Christians, has taken swift action to drive the business out of the area. They have met, planned strategy, and are now picketing the store daily. They are determined to win. It is an exciting example of the zeal of decent people who want to rid their community of one type of ungodliness.

But, at the same time, I wonder if we give the same energies and enthusiasm to deeds of compassion? Are we as eager to do good as we are to defeat evil?

Our love for God is shown in our compassionate relationship to others. In the parable of the good Samaritan, the motivation to respond to the injured man's need is crucial. The Samaritan not only saw, but was moved by a compassionate heart.

Looking in the opposite direction, we see the Pharisees, who were pious and worked hard at keeping the letter of the law and made sure that others knew it. But Jesus accused the Pharisees of being phony, filthy tombs. They looked good on the outside, but were rotten on the inside. Their hearts were stone; they had no compassion for the rest of humanity. Jesus calls us to be *lovers,* not *legalists.*

In Philippians 2:19-22, we find one of our best examples of a caring Christian: Timothy. Paul says of him, "I have no one like him, who will be genuinely anxious for your welfare. They all look after their own interests, not those of Jesus Christ" (vv. 20-21) If only we could be like Timothy!

Our best example of compassion is the Lord Jesus himself, who said, as he looked over Jerusalem, "O Jerusalem, Jerusalem, killing the prophets and stoning those who are sent to you! How often would I have gathered your children together as a hen gathers her brood under her wings, and you would not!" (Luke 13:34).

Another good example of Jesus' compassion is the feeding of the five thousand (Mark 6:30-44). Jesus and his disciples were tired and hungry, and yet when Jesus saw a great throng of people, "He had compassion on them, because they were like sheep without a shepherd" (v. 34). Even when the disciples had clearly had enough and were ready to send the people away, Jesus was still concerned about the needs of the people.

I am concerned about our government leaders, many of whom may have other good qualities, but often seem to lack compassion. In order to even enter any of the major political races, a candidate is almost required to be a person of great influence and great affluence. Many have long since forgotten, if they ever knew, what it was to be without the necessities of life. They look out over the needs of our people with hearts of stone. The purpose of government is not simply a welfare service, but it scares me to think that some of the leaders we have chosen exhibit so little real compassion for others.

Compassion is central to one of the two greatest commandments, which Jesus himself gave: "The second is this, 'You shall love your neighbor as yourself.' There is no other commandment greater than these" (Mark 12:31). In our self-centeredness, we often feel sorry for ourselves. But Jesus said that we should hurt for others in their problems and sufferings in the same way we hurt for ourselves. If it were in our power to stop it, none of us would allow ourselves and our families to starve. And yet, we are content to eat well and let our neighbors starve. Where is our compassion?

A compassionate heart is important to our discipleship, but without hands that let go, it is incomplete. Once we see and feel, we must act.

"For the poor will never cease out of the land; therefore I command you, You shall open wide your hand to your brother, to the needy and to the poor, in the land" (Deut. 15:11).

A virtuous woman is also described as one who "opens her hand to the poor, and reaches out her hands to the needy" (Prov. 31:20).

Letting go is difficult. We struggle for security in a world that is constantly changing. We've been through some bad economic times: high unemployment and high inflation. We want to hold on to what we have and accumulate more for a rainy day. But if this becomes our philosophy, will we ever have enough? Will we become like the man who tore down his old barns and built larger ones to house his increasing goods with no thought for the needy of his day?

We must allow the Lord to help us break the hold that materialism has on us. Only as we are liberated from that bondage will we be able to truly let go. It does not necessarily mean getting rid of our possessions. It does mean an attitude which allows us to part with things easily or not have them in the first place. It is a God-given attitude that focuses on people rather than things.

Our eyes, our hearts, our hands—we need to give ourselves to the Lord, and His Spirit will guide our giving. These words of Paul give us a good illustration.

> We want you to know, brethren, about the grace of God which has been shown in the churches of Macedonia, for in a severe test of affliction, their abundance of joy and their extreme poverty have overflowed in a wealth of liberality on their part. For they gave according to their means, as I can testify, and beyond their means, of their own free will, begging us earnestly for the favor of taking part in the relief of the saints—and this, not as we expected, but first they gave themselves to the Lord and to us by the will of God (2 Cor. 8:1-5).

Notice that these Christians gave beyond their means, more than they could afford, we might say, in order to share with fellow Christians. (In case you hadn't noticed, there's that word *sacrifice* written between the lines.) They also gave freely—no one said they had to or else. Now look at the next phrase, "begging us earnestly for the favor of taking part." They were excited about giving! They were eager to give. What a spirit! What if we were all like that?

And in the last clause, we see the reason for their generosity. We see why they were able to give with little thought for themselves. They had *first* given *themselves* to the Lord as is God's will for each of us. Eyes, hearts, hands, their whole being was consecrated to God.

Some of us are still holding back some of the departments of our lives from the Lord. One of these departments is money. Are we still holding the purse strings? Are we able to let go and let the Holy Spirit take control of our lives in this area?

---

1. Howard P. Colson, *The Practical Message of James,* (Nashville: Broadman Press, 1969), p. 24.

What Can We Do?

Wealth is a sacred trust which its possessor is bound to administer in his lifetime for the good of the community.
—Andrew Carnegie

As we have already said, the first and most important thing we can do is to open our eyes and ears to the needs around us. Most of us don't really hear when needs are expressed by individuals we know, much less those we don't know. I am constantly hearing about needs I can help meet among friends and acquaintances. I am sure all of us are having those same experiences whether or not we respond. I am often told that people are too proud to accept help, so why offer? I find this largely untrue, if we are tactful and acting in love. I believe it is one of our many excuses for not helping others.

There are avenues for stewardship and service in our personal lives, in our churches, in our communities, and in our world. Let us examine a few of the possibilities in each area.

In Our Personal Lives

There are countless ways that we can minister as individuals and families to the needs around us. The following list will get us started, but it just scratches the surface of the realm of possibilities for those of us who would try to "love our neighbors as ourselves."

1. Invite newlyweds into your home for a meal toward the end of the month when their funds might be running low.

2. Invite the new homemaker in for a coffee/tea break and get acquainted.

3. Be a spiritual welcome wagon for newcomers. Bring a meal or a loaf of homemade bread the day they move in. Offer to help arrange furniture or wash dishes as they are unpacked. Provide baby-sitting during the hectic moving-in period.

4. Offer to help tutor children who need it.

5. Provide emergency child care during times of death or accident.

6. When death strikes, offer your help specifically. Offer to do laundry, run an errand, or bring supper. Always be ready to listen.

7. Send greeting cards and notes to the ill and handicapped. Bring a magazine or a book that might suit the person's interest. Help with chores or run errands. Offer to write a letter for the person who is sick.

8. Take disadvantaged children on a short trip with your family to the zoo, pool, or for a picnic. Bring these children to your church children's choir practice (with parent's permission of course).

9. Go through your family's clothing regularly and sort out unusable or unworn clothing to give to your

church clothing bank or to give to someone you know personally who could use them.

10. Gather up unused or outgrown toys to give to disadvantaged children in your community.

11. Give a single parent a day/night out: offer babysitting.

12. Bring a meal to a senior citizen. Call in advance.

13. Bring cookies or a loaf of homemade bread to a senior citizen and visit. Take note of dietary needs.

14. Be aware of transients, college students, and the lonely. Include them in your family activities from time to time. Remember their birthdays with a card. An occasional telephone call would be appreciated, too.

15. Should a local disaster occur, adopt a family or individual temporarily. Sleep and food provisions are the first necessities. Later you could help people file insurance claims. Give them hope for the future.

In Our Churches

We can respond to the needs of individuals in our churches as they come to our attention.

Start and support a food closet and clothes closet in your church if there is not one. If your church has one, you can help to keep it well stocked. Then be aware of families and individuals who could be helped by it.

Listen for job openings that may suit the unemployed in your church. Then contact the unemployed about the job openings and help them in any way possible. For example, secure a job application for them or provide transportation to the interview if needed.

Support your church benevolence fund. Speak for increasing the benevolence item in your church budget and decreasing the more selfish and materialistic items in your budget.

Be active in educating church members about world hunger. Take an active role in promoting a world hunger day in your church. Help educate your church members about your denomination's giving plan. Show what it is doing here and around the world to meet the urgent needs of our neighbors.

Give sacrificially through your church to meet these desperate needs.

Lead in local mission action projects following a survey to determine needs.

In the case of a local disaster, your church could provide a place to sleep and food on a temporary basis.

Cooperate with other agencies in a hunger relief ministry. Know what agencies to call on for help. Be ready to help those agencies in return with community food banks, soup kitchens, and so forth.

Set ministries to help the elderly poor in your church. Provide services such as building, repairing, cooking, and so forth.

Find areas in your church community where there are pockets of need. Where there is hunger, provide immediate temporary relief. Check with families for food likes and dislikes and special dietary needs. Identify clothing needs and sizes and then have a churchwide clothing party to help supply these needs. Do the same with toys where there are children involved. If there are basic furniture needs, the church family can help locate the items needed by checking in their own homes and Goodwill stores, and so forth.

In Our Communities

If your community has some type guide to human resources, get one and become familiar with community resources for helping people. When needs arise, direct or take the person to the appropriate agency.

Find out how you can help the agencies to do their jobs. Can they use volunteers? If so, how? What could you do?

Take on a poor family or individual that you can help provide for on a regular basis. Thanksgiving baskets are good, but none of us could get by a whole year on a Thanksgiving basket. We like to eat in January and July, too. Check with your local board of assistance for names of eligible families. The board can connect you with the right person or family in strictest confidentiality. Try it, you'll be blessed.

In Our World

Obviously, the needs on a worldwide scale are great. The possibilities are inexhaustible.

There are many organizations, both Christian and secular, that exist to help the needy in the world. It is not an easy task to decide which of the many organizations will best serve our purposes in giving.

We all want to give our money to organizations that will use our money responsibly for justice and the advancement of God's kingdom. As we seek out such organizations, there are many questions that we might ask.

—Which causes are most important to me?

—Which organizations can I trust?

—How much of the money I give goes for overhead and how much really helps meet the needs of people?

—How can I tell if the organizations are doing what they say? Which ones are not?

—Which organizations need my money most?

—What are this organization's theological and political stances? How important are they?

—Should I give to Christian groups only, or are there others that are doing important work as well?

—Should I seek out organizations that in a spirit of compassion are helping people *now?* Or should I look for groups whose purpose is fundamental, long-term, social, and political change?

—What is its view of God and God's creation? What is its attitude about humanity?

—Does it challenge the structures of oppression or support them?

—What is the nature of its activities? Is it in keeping with the spirit of Jesus?

There are some other questions we should ask before becoming involved in a major giving program concerning the organizational management.

—When was the organization founded?

—How large is their paid staff?

—What are the highest and lowest paid salaries on the staff?

—Who makes the decisions? Are the decision makers all white? Are they all male?

—How is the organization governed?

—Is there government support of influence?

—Is there strong denominational influence or support?

There are many organizations with a multitude of worthy purposes that ask our help.[1]

We could divide the organizations into two main groups: Christian and secular. Secular organizations serve for purely humanitarian reasons while Christian groups serve the needs of people for the cause of Christ. Some groups are Christian in name only and function as secular social service agencies on the field.

Of the Christian organizations, some are evangelical and others are not. Denominational mission boards would come at the top of the list of evangelical agencies. However, there are evangelical relief programs that are not affiliated with any one denomination.

The purposes and actions of these organizations are many. Some provide hunger and disaster relief. Some work for social and economic development and attempt to eliminate the root causes of hunger and injustice. Some seek political status quo while others are reformists, involved in political action. Some groups minister to prisoners and their families and work for justice. Some respond to emergencies; others undertake developmental projects. Some agencies call for radical economic sharing. Some fight disease and poor sanitation. Some organizations serve refugee relief and resettlement. Some organizations choose a single cause such as publishing, translating, selling, and promoting the Bible. Some groups are involved in child sponsorship and educational efforts. Some groups promote peace and oppose militarism and weapons buildup. Some organizations promote Bible study and evangelism.

One organization states their reason for being this way:

> We believe in the God-imputed dignity of each individual. Poverty, destitution, and alienation from the mainstream of life mutilate the human spirit and bind the soul in darkness. But we dare not help suffering people apart from the church because it is in this relationship that the whole need of suffering people is met.[2]

The *whole* need of the world's suffering people cannot be met with food or medical supplies or development. Meeting their total needs must include sharing Christ.

---

1. For a good, but not exhaustive list, see "A Giver's Guide," *The Other Side,* March 1983.
2. "A Giver's Guide," *The Other Side,* March 1983.

The Challenge Before Us

Let us show how he has changed us,
And remade us as his own.[1]

Every December I thrill to see *A Christmas Carol* by Charles Dickens or *Scrooge,* the more recent film adaptation on television. I enjoy seeing a man, who was as miserly as we can possibly imagine, have a change of heart and startle everyone with his newfound generosity. I love it when he gives good gifts to his previously mistreated employee, Bob Cratchit, and his family, and offers to help dear, little Tiny Tim. I love it when he renews an almost dead relationship with his nephew and his family. I love it when his Christmas "Humbug!" turns to Christmas happiness.

I think I enjoy it so much because, to some extent, it is my story. Hopefully, I wasn't as tragic a figure as Ebenezer Scrooge, but still I was professing Christ and living for myself. I was using the other nine tenths for me and my family without a great deal of regard for what the Lord wanted me to do with it. It bothered me that there were needy people in the world, but not enough to do anything about it. In my experience, there were no nighttime visitors or trips into the past, present, or future. But, just the same, the Lord did speak to me in a life-changing way, and as the song suggests He's not finished with us yet.

One Saturday afternoon, not being much of a skater, I sat in a skating rink reading a book while my husband and daughter made their way repeatedly around the floor. I'll never forget that day. I was beginning to read a new book, *Starving in the Shadow of Plenty,* by Loretta Schwartz-Nobel. I don't know exactly why I even checked it out from the library although I've always been rather interested in social problems. I know now that the Lord had His hand in it. Because as I sat there reading about Martha Roca and other people in this country who have died hungry and alone, tears began to roll down my face. I started to see myself as the Christian I really was. I had all that I needed, and I had ignored the need in my community, my country, my world. *I* was part of the problem.

From that moment the Lord began to change the direction of my life. The transformation may not have been as apparent to the world as was Scrooge's amazing turn, but it was nonetheless very real. My attitudes and goals began to change; I started to look at life differently. I was becoming more of that new creation that God had intended me to be back in 1954 when I accepted Christ as Savior. I wanted to shout to the world, "Something has happened to me!"

God had used this book by Loretta Schwartz-Nobel as a tool in giving a new beginning to an "old" Christian. Waldo Werning reminds us in his book, *The Steward-*

ship Call: "Only God can keep us aware of our calling and opportunities to serve him. He alone can motivate us for our calling or revive us when we become weary.[2]

Since then, the Lord has touched me in countless ways: through sermons, through books, through experiences with people, and through His Word. Scriptures on giving and concern for others have literally jumped out at me continually from the pages of the Bible. Werner speaks of the value of God's Word in bringing us to new levels of Christian growth: "The Word will reveal where there is a theological gap in programs, a dichotomy between theology and practice, aspiration and actuality, message and method. It is possible for people to motivate other people, but God gives us his Word, to call one another to repentance and to renew us for his covenant plan."[3] In my case, there was certainly a dichotomy between theology and practice when it came to this question of caring and giving. I suspect it is true of other Christians as well.

I discovered for myself what I should have known all along, what I had only verbalized before: that the lordship of Christ changes our attitudes toward others and our attitudes about money and possessions in a profound way.

I discovered that, in living for myself, however unconsciously, I was defeating my purpose of giving testimony to Christ. Who could believe that I could belong to one who was totally selfless? The credibility gap would be just too great!

I discovered that I had taken what I wanted from

Jesus' teachings but rejected his life-style. I had accepted his salvation, I prayed, worshiped, read my Bible, went to Sunday School, even tithed. But I wouldn't deny myself. Certainly, I could be a Christian without doing that!

I discovered that in giving only lip service to our Lord's command to love our neighbors as ourselves, I was the one described in James 2:14-17, saying, "Go in peace, be warmed and filled," without seriously attempting to meet the need. The saying, "Put your money where your mouth is" contains much truth for those of us who would pay lip service to genuine concern for others. Ministering to others does not always require money, but our money can help to break the credibility gap in a world where millions of overindulgent North Americans go on diets and millions of people in other countries go the way of slow starvation.

In short, with the Lord's help, I discovered the Pharisee in me in the area of stewardship. The self-righteousness of the Pharisees is so apparent to us, yet, it is difficult to see our own. I know that in the future the Lord will show me new areas that he can change in accordance with his will.

I expect that in 1954 I accepted Jesus as Savior, which is a good beginning, but not as Lord of my life. It is difficult, especially as a child, to understand all that that decision entails. Even as adults, our understanding is only partial (1 Cor. 13:9). I am still growing toward that goal of making Jesus Lord of my life. It is not easy. We all prefer an easy religion, but because

Christianity is not a man-made religion, rather a relationship with the Son of God himself, we cannot expect it on our own terms.

Along the way, we can hope to reach plateaus as we allow the Holy Spirit to lead us. For me, this experience has been an important plateau, but, I hasten to say, not a stopping point. This book comes from an overwhelming desire to share what God has done in my own life in this area, with the hope that He will use it to speak to your heart also. God used a book to begin a change in me.

We can change the *externals* in our lives like how often we go to church, the color of our hair, the way we walk, what kind of movies we see, or the kind of clothes we wear. God through His Spirit changes the heart, the *internals*. When God changes the heart, then, and only then, do we experience really significant changes in our lives. Waldo Werning writes: "The Holy Spirit is the Great Transformer. He changes weakness to power, bad dispositions to pleasant attitudes, self-centeredness to Christ-likeness, self-reasoning to Christ-mindedness.[4]

Our salvation experience, for most of us, is an event in our past. It is our assurance of eternal life with our Creator and Savior and of victorious living here on earth. But God warns us through His prophet, Isaiah, that we must not dwell too heavily on what He has done for us now. "Remember not the former things, nor consider the things of old. Behold, I am doing a new thing" (Isa. 43:18-19*a*). The challenge is that we let God do something new in us, that we let our Lord change our old attitudes and old ways when they have become like rigid wineskins, unable to contain the new wine of the gospel.

We live in a lopsided world where a few have everything and many have nothing. Christians can change that if they will. There is nothing Christian about extremes of wealth and poverty. Loretta Schwartz-Nobel concludes:

> The answers will come from the action each of us takes and the responsibilities that each of us assumes. It means not forgetting as I forgot. It means not allowing our neighbors to forget. It means reaching our political leaders. It means implementing things and having the discipline, the judgment, and the strength of purpose to follow them until they are accomplished. The options are still ours. We can care for ourselves, each other, and the earth together OR we can destroy what is left.[5]

Christians can live like the world like spoiled children. Or we can allow the vertical relationship with our Creator and Lord to affect the horizontal relationships that we have with His people.

Our Lord can empower us to throw off *religion* and put on *relationship.* He calls us to be a dynamic people, not a static one. He will help us to *believe* what we *say* and *do* what we *believe.* In the final reckoning, one great truth stands out. *"What we really believe, we do. Everything else is just so much religious rhetoric."*[6]

---

1. From "We Are Called to Be God's People," by Thomas A. Jackson, 1973.
2. Werning, p. 52.
3. Werning, pp. 51-52.
4. Werning, p. 28.
5. Loretta Schwartz-Nobel, *Starving in the Shadow of Plenty* (New York: Putnam, 1981), p. 226.
6. World Relief, "State of World Needs in the 80s" (Wheaton, Ill.: World Relief, 1983), p. 19.